T4-AVE-835

PN
4738
.K76
1987

Kronenwetter,
 Michael.

Politics and the
press

$12.90

DATE		
	JUN 1990	

THE CHICAGO PUBLIC LIBRARY

WOODSON REGIONAL
LIBRARY CENTER
9525 SOUTH HALSTED STREET
CHICAGO, ILLINOIS 60628

© THE BAKER & TAYLOR CO.

Politics and the Press

Michael Kronenwetter

POLITICS AND THE PRESS

Issues in American
History

Franklin Watts
New York/London/Toronto
Sydney/1987

Photographs courtesy of
The Bettmann Archive: pp. 14, 17, 21, 33, 36, 39, 49, 65, 67, 69;
New York Public Library, Schomberg Collection: p. 48;
AP/Wide World: pp. 77, 96, 102, 115, 123;
LBJ Library: p. 82;
UPI/Bettmann Newsphotos: p. 107;
ABC Newsphoto: p. 119.

Library of Congress Cataloging-in-Publication Data

Kronenwetter, Michael.
Politics and the press.

(Issues in American history)
Includes index.
Summary: Discusses the sometimes difficult
relationship between politics and the press, covering
such issues as freedom of the press, editorial fairness,
and press endorsement of political candidates, as
reflected in American history.
1. Government and the press—United States—Juvenile
literature.   2. Press and politics—United States—
Juvenile literature.   [1. Government and the press—
History.   2. Press and politics—History]   I. Title.
II. Series.
PN4738.K76   1987   302.2'32'0973   86-24228
ISBN 0-531-10333-1

Copyright © 1987 by Michael Kronenwetter
All rights reserved
Printed in the United States of America
6   5   4   3   2   1

R00719 70846

Contents

The Key to Power—Establishing Freedom of the Press

When the press is free,
and every man able to read,
all is safe.

Thomas Jefferson

J ohann Gutenberg and his fellow printers of the fifteenth century were not politicians. They were tradesmen and artisans. They probably never dreamed, when they first developed movable type to enable them to print faster, that they were changing the nature of politics forever. But they were. Without meaning to, or even understanding what they were doing, they were helping to make modern political democracy possible.

The Beginnings of the Press
The basic idea of democracy is very old. It dates back at least to ancient Greece, if not before. But modern democracy—in which the people of a large and diverse society can each have a voice in the way that society is run—only became possible after the development of the printing press. In order for enormous numbers of people, spread across large countries, to participate in their governments, they needed information. In order for them to receive it, a means had to be found that could disseminate information rapidly and uniformly to large numbers of people. It was the printing press that provided the first such means of mass communication, the newssheet.

The printing press did not create modern democratic institutions, nor did it cause the revolutions that first established them. But it helped to spread the concept of democracy among the people, both in France and in the American colonies of England. And it was the press that kept the people informed of political developments. Without it, the American, French and other revolutions that eventually brought democratic government to much of the world could not have taken place in the ways they did. And without the printing press, the governments those revolutions established would have been very different.

The press, then, played an important role in the very formation of modern political life. And the press—a term that now includes radio, television and other news media as well as the printed press—has continued to exercise enormous political power ever since.

The British Traditions
In the beginning, printing presses were used mostly by governments or by private businesses under government control. Each of these already powerful elements of society used the printing press to enhance its power even further. Governments used it to advertise their achievements, and thus to promote patriotism and loyalty. Businesses used it to advertise their products and to raise their profits. Because of their virtual monopoly on the presses, both government and business exercised great influence over what was printed, and therefore over what information the public received.

The governments of the time kept strict control of what was printed. As early as 1534, for example, British printers had to get a license for each item they wanted to print. If a proposed publication was disagreeable to the government, the license would be refused. In several countries, the press was regarded as little more than a servant of the government. Printers were put on the government payroll and paid both to print what the government wanted printed and *not* to print what the government preferred to keep hidden.

Most printers simply accepted this situation. They were businessmen, after all, and they were happy to do whatever the government would pay them to do. Other printers, however, chafed under the restrictions and tried to get around them. Some of them did so for economic reasons. They resented paying the license fees. Others did so because they wanted to use their presses to express political views. Since those views were often critical of the government, they could not obtain licenses to publish them.

This was particularly true in England, where the beginnings of parliamentary democracy had already been established, and public opinion was recognized as a significant element in national political life. Since the press was the most powerful organ available for influencing, and manipulating, public opinion, critics of the government were eager to use its power for their own ends. The government, of course, was equally eager to keep control of it.

In 1632, when King Charles I found it impossible to regulate the contents of the newssheets, he banned them altogether. Nine years later, the British Parliament, which was locked in a power struggle with the king, forced him to lift the ban and allow the newssheets to resume publishing. But Parliament immediately moved to take control of the press itself, and used it to consolidate its own power.

It was at this time, when there was no real freedom of the press in England, that the first great argument for such freedom was published. Its author was the poet, John Milton. Opposed both to the king's ban on the press and to Parliament's regulation of it, he argued in his *Areopagitica* in 1644 that citizens should be free "to know, to utter, and to argue freely," in print as well as in speech.

It was not until 1695, however, that the government finally stopped licensing newspapers. Even then, it did not entirely relinquish its control over them. Tension between the press and the government continued in England, as it did in virtually every other country. Even such a famous writer as Daniel Defoe, the author of *Robinson Crusoe,* was jailed for publishing a satire critical of the government.

The major weapon used by the British government to intimidate the press was the law of "seditious libel." This law made it a crime to publish a libel against the government. A libel was defined as anything that aroused hostility or resentment against the government. That definition covered virtually any criticism of the government, as well as the publication of any information that might discredit it. What is more, courts ruled that information could be considered libelous even if it was true. One court held that a true libel against the government was even worse than a false one. The truth, after all, was more likely to harm the government than a lie. The truth could not be disproved.

The government also used economic measures to silence press criticisms. It passed a Stamp Act, which put a tax on newspapers, and imposed duties on the advertisements that appeared in them. When the printers showed signs of becoming too independent, the government put pressure on them by raising these taxes and duties.

Britain's American colonies, then, were the heirs to two very different press traditions. The first was the tradition of the press as a servant of the government. The second was that of the press as a weapon with which to criticize the government. Behind both traditions, however, there was a single awareness. The press had an enormous power to influence public opinion, and thereby to influence political events. That power would soon be convincingly demonstrated in the American colonies themselves.

The Press in the Colonies

Things did not start out well for the concept of freedom of the press in Britain's American colonies. The very first newspaper there, *Public Occurrences Both Forreign and Domestick*, was immediately suppressed because it was critical of the British army in Massachusetts. There would not be another paper published in the colonies for more than a decade. When the next paper finally did appear, in 1704, it was printed with the approval—and under the control—of the colonial government.

The first independent colonial paper to survive for any length of time was the *New-England Courant*, which was first published by James Franklin in 1721. It was even more critical of the colonial government than *Publick Occurrences* had been, and Franklin was soon thrown into jail. His imprisonment did not mean the end of the paper, however, since his sixteen-year-old brother, Benjamin, took over his duties. It was not a coincidence that Ben Franklin was both a printer and a revolutionary.

Newspapers soon sprang up all over the colonies. Many of them were little more than creatures of the government. But some, like the *Courant*, were independent. These papers tended to be organs for business or political interests that had grievances against the government, and were often critical of the way the colonies were being run. Not surprisingly, the colonial governments did everything they could to suppress them.

This proved harder to do in the eighteenth century than it had been in the seventeenth. By the mid-1700s, many colonists already considered themselves politically, culturally and economically oppressed by the mother government in England, and by its colonial ser-

Young Benjamin Franklin worked in his brother's printing establishment, publishing the first successful independent newspaper in the American colonies.

vants in America. This growing resentment found a public voice in the independent American press, and a new spirit of resistance grew up against the government's efforts to muzzle it.

Things came to a head in August of 1735, when the government of the colony of New York brought a printer named Zenger to trial for seditious libel. More than any other single event, his trial would lay the foundation for freedom of the press in America.

The Right to Complain

John Peter Zenger was the publisher of the *New York Weekly Journal*. His paper was financially supported by a political faction opposed to the government of the colony of New York, and to its head, Governor William Cosby. Echoing the views of its supporters, the *Journal* was vehement in its attacks on Cosby.

Zenger was a recent immigrant from Germany and his English was poor. Consequently, it is unlikely that he wrote these attacks himself. They were probably written by members of the faction that supported the *Journal*. Nonetheless, Zenger was the paper's publisher, and as such he was legally responsible for whatever appeared in it.

Cosby tried at least twice to get grand juries to indict Zenger for seditious libel. The juries were made up of ordinary colonists, however, and they refused. Whether this was an indication of the popularity of the press in New York or of the *un*popularity of Cosby's government is not clear. In any case, having failed to persuade the grand juries, Cosby went over their heads to the executive council of the colony and had it issue a warrant for Zenger's arrest.

The publisher was held in jail for more than eight months before he was brought to trial. When the trial finally began, it became clear that the government was willing to go to virtually any lengths to convict him. When Zenger's lawyers objected to the fact that the judge in the case was a political crony of Governor Cosby, the judge dismissed the lawyers. They were replaced by an aging but still brilliant lawyer from Philadelphia named Andrew Hamilton.

Hamilton turned the trial into a debate on freedom of the press. He attacked the traditional European view of the press as a servant of government. Instead, he offered a new and very American idea of a press whose right it was to exposè the truth, however much that truth hurt those in power.

A key element in the defense was the argument that truth should be a defense against libel. Admitting that what Zenger had printed was damaging to the government, the lawyer argued that the jury should find him innocent anyway—for the simple reason that what he had printed was true. "Truth ought to govern in the whole affair of libels," he declared. "I beg leave to insist, that the right of complaining or remonstrating is natural." The only restraint upon that natural right, he insisted, should be the law, and the law should only restrain "what is false." This was a radical idea. It struck at the fundamental assumptions that lay behind the law of seditious libel. Among them was the belief that government was above the truth: that if the truth would hurt the government, the truth had to be concealed. That assumption was based on the idea that the government was not just more important than the truth, it was more important than the people.

"It is said and insisted upon by Mr. Attorney that government is a sacred thing; that it is to be supported and reverenced," Hamilton told the jury. "[I]t is the government that protects our persons and estates; that

John Peter Zenger stands in the dock at
his famous trial for libel while his
lawyer, Andrew Hamilton, argues his case.

prevents treasons, murders, robberies, riots, and all the train of evils that overturns kingdoms and states and ruins particular persons; and if those in the administration, especially the supreme magistrate, must have all their conduct censured by private men, government cannot subsist."

What he was describing was not just the view of the prosecution. It was the view of the government. It was the law both in Britain and in her colonies, a law based on a real fear. If the commoners who wrote for the newspapers were free to complain and criticize the government, what would happen to the authority of the state? Not just the individuals who ran the government, but the government itself might be brought into ridicule. The people might even begin to question the right of the government to govern. Such a thing was, as Hamilton described the government's view, "a licentiousness not to be tolerated. . . . [I]t brings the rulers of the people into contempt, and their authority not to be regarded, and so in the end the laws cannot be put into execution."

But, argued Hamilton, the real cause of such evils was not the newspapers, but the "abuse of power" by those in authority. It was not the fact that the newspapers complained about that abuse, but the abuse itself, that "commonly brought [the rulers] into contempt with the people." If Cosby was regarded with contempt, it was because of his own actions. Zenger had only exposed those actions, he was not responsible for them. Cosby was.

The effort to prosecute Zenger was the typical response of an oppressive government. "Men who injure and oppress the people under their administration provoke them to cry out and complain; and then make that very complaint the foundation for new oppres-

sions and persecutions," Hamilton explained. He urged the jury to lay a new and "noble foundation for securing to ourselves, our posterity, and our neighbors, that to which nature and the laws of our country have given us a right—the liberty, both of exposing and opposing arbitrary power (in these parts of the world, at least), by speaking and writing truth."

The jury did. It took them only minutes to declare Zenger innocent of libel. In doing so, they agreed with Hamilton that government was *not* sacred in America, and was *not* to be reverenced; that the press and the people had a right to complain and remonstrate about the actions of their government. Most importantly, they agreed that—"in these parts of the world, at least"—the press would be free to expose and oppose arbitrary power by writing the truth.

Stirring Up Revolt

The fear felt by the prosecution in the Zenger case—the fear of "all the train of evils that overturns kingdoms and states"—was not unfounded. A portion of the colonial press was soon calling for just such an overturn. But, as Hamilton had suggested, the government did much to bring its troubles on itself.

In 1765, Britain passed a new Stamp Act—this one aimed at the colonies in America. Without asking the colonial legislatures for their consent, the British government placed taxes on virtually all printed materials. These included legal documents, advertisements and, of course, newspapers. The Stamp Act raised a greater storm of opposition than had ever been seen in the colonies. Virtually everyone was against it, and among its strongest opponents were the editors of newspapers. Most newspapers were also printing shops, and the taxes affected all branches of their business.

Even several editors who had been nonpolitical before, at least in print, now used their newspapers to
complain bitterly about Britain's action. Three entirely
new papers were founded specifically to attack the act.
From that time on, colonial papers would be in the
forefront of the opposition to Britain's authority, and
they would play a major role in preparing the American public for revolution.

The *Boston Gazette*, for example, numbered among
its writers such revolutionaries as Samuel and John
Adams, and John Hancock. It is said that the Boston
Tea Party was planned in the *Gazette*'s offices, and that
the participants gathered there to put on their Indian
disguises. Excerpts from Thomas Paine's pamphlet,
Common Sense, were reprinted in papers all over the
colonies. More than any other single document, it per-
suaded many Americans that a break with Britain was
necessary.

The colonial press was far from unanimous in its
support for revolution. There were many loyalist
newspapers as well, and still others that tried to remain neutral, publishing both sides of the great debate. But it was ultimately the proindependence press
that prevailed.

The Patriot Press, as it was called, did not cause the
American Revolution. That was caused by the grievances of the colonists, both real and imagined, and by
Britain's bungling and insensitivity. But the press did
help to stir up anger against Britain, and to build sympathy for the idea of independence. And once the revolution began, it helped to keep up the revolutionaries'
morale, even in the darkest days when it seemed sure
that Britain would win.

More dramatically than anything that had happened before, either in Europe or in the colonies, the

The TIMES are Dreadful, Dismal, Doleful, Dolorous, and DOLLAR-LESS.

An Emblem of the Effects of the STAMP. O! the fatal Stamp.

Thursday, October 31, 1765

THE

Pennsylvania Journal;
AND
WEEKLY ADVERTISER

NUMB. 1195.

EXPIRING: In Hopes of a Resurrection to LIFE again.

I AM sorry to be obliged to acquaint my Readers, that as The STAMP-Act, is fear'd to be obligatory upon us after the First of November en-suing, (the fatal To morrow) the Publisher of this Paper unable to bear the Burthen, has thought it expedient TO STOP awhile, in order to deliberate, whether any Methods can be found to elude the Chains forged for us, and escape the insupportable Slavery, which it is hoped, from the last Representations now made against that Act, may be effected. Mean while, I must earnestly Request every Individual of my Subscribers many of whom have been long behind Hand, that they would immediately Discharge their respective Arrears that I may be able, not only to support myself during the Interval, but be better prepared to proceed again with this Paper, whenever an opening for that Purpose appears, which I hope will be soon. WILLIAM BRADFORD

This Pennsylvania newspaper, a victim of the Stamp Act,
was forced to stop publication because its publisher
could not afford the tax required by the oppressive law.

American Revolution demonstrated the enormous power of the press to influence political events. Governments had long feared that power without fully recognizing the extent of it. Now that extent was clear to everyone.

America's successful revolution sent fear through many European courts. If revolution could happen in America, might it happen in Europe too? And part of this fear was fear of the press—the press that had fomented revolution and spurred the people to rebellion against lawful authority.

What had taken place in America, then, made most European governments even more wary of the press than they had been before. It made them more determined than ever to restrict the press's freedom. In the new United States of America, however, the government moved in the opposite direction.

The First Amendment

Instead of taking steps to restrict the press, America's founders began by taking steps to restrict the government itself. The very first amendment to the new Constitution forbade the government from exercising any control over the press. "Congress shall make no law," declared the amendment, "abridging the freedom of speech or of the press." No government on earth had ever dared to guarantee the press such freedom.

The First Amendment was not supported by all the founders, however. Many of them feared the power of a completely free press. After all, a power that could rally the people in a good cause, such as they believed the revolution had been, could rally people in a bad cause as well.

It was not long, in fact, before even some of those who had supported the First Amendment came to regret having done so. Regret was particularly strong among the members of the Federalist party. They were soon angered by the attacks made on them by newspapers favoring the rival Democratic-Republican party. In order to silence their opponents in 1798, the Federalists, who controlled Congress, passed the Alien and Sedition Acts, one of which was specifically designed to muzzle the press. This act made it a crime to write, print or utter false, scandalous or malicious statements against the government (which meant, in effect, the Federalists), or to bring them "into contempt or disrepute." It was the old law of seditious libel all over again, only worse. It even forbade American citizens to conspire "to oppose any measure or measures of the government of the United States."

The Sedition Act seemed clearly in conflict with the First Amendment—as well as with the general principles of political freedom and representative democracy on which the new country had been founded. Nevertheless, it remained in effect until March of 1801, and several editors were actually jailed under it. And, although many people consider it a major violation of the constitutional guarantee of freedom of the press, it was never actually ruled unconstitutional. In any case, it failed to silence opposition to the Federalists. In the next national election, Thomas Jefferson, a Democratic Republican, was elected president. He promptly pardoned all the journalists who had been found guilty under the act.

The Sedition Act of 1798 was probably the most direct and successful attack on the freedom of the press in American history, but it was not the last. There have been many others. But, while some of these attacks have intimidated the press, and have even temporarily silenced some elements of it, none have ultimately succeeded in overturning the principle of freedom of the press enshrined in the First Amendment. That ideal of freedom has occasionally been violated, but it has never been abandoned, by either the press or the government.

Still, press freedom is not absolute, even in the United States. There are legal restrictions on the press, some of which will be discussed later in this book. But those restrictions are generally acknowledged to be fewer—particularly where the publication of information and opinion involving the government is concerned—than those in any other country. Even in the mother country of England, stricter libel laws, as well as laws limiting what can be printed about the activities of the courts, among others, act as greater checks on the press's freedom.

It is its freedom, more than anything else, that has given the American press its enormous power to influence political events. In the chapters that follow, we will examine some of the ways in which the press has used that power.

2

Molding a Press, Molding a Nation

The penny papers
of New York do more
to govern this country
than the White House
at Washington.

Wendell Phillips,
reformer

The new nation and its constitutionally protected press grew up together. The press, in fact, helped to mold the new nation, just as the nation's ideals of freedom helped to mold a new kind of press. From the beginning, American newspapers were used as vehicles for political opinion. All the great issues that were raised in the attempt to establish a new form of government on this continent were thrashed out in the nation's newspapers.

Setting a Course
The convention that drew up the United States Constitution was held in secret in 1787, but the questions it discussed were of enormous public concern. It was the newspapers that provided the medium for the public debate over the form that the new government should take. When three of the Founding Fathers, Alexander Hamilton, James Madison and John Jay, laid out the basic principles on which the Constitution would be based in a famous series of essays known as *The Federalist Papers*, those essays were first published in the New York newspapers. When it came time for the individual states to decide whether to ratify the Constitution, the battle was often fought out in the states' newspapers before being resolved in the legislatures.

For the most part, the early papers presented their political arguments in the form of letters. Sometimes these letters appeared over the name of a prominent citizen. Often, they appeared over a pseudonym. (Pseudonyms were common in eighteenth-century America. The authors of *The Federalist Papers*, for example, signed themselves with the Latin name "Publius.") Eventually, papers began to print what are now called "editorials," formal statements of opinion on political and other matters, which were presented as the official positions of the newspaper itself. In some cases, these editorials represented the personal views of the paper's editor. In other cases, they represented the views of the financial interests that supported the newspaper, and that, in effect, told the editor what to print. Whatever the source of the views expressed, their expression helped to shape the views of the paper's readers.

The Partisan Press

Many of the newspapers of the early nineteenth century were the children of political parties. That is, they were founded either by a political party, or by an advocate of a party, and were used to promote its interests. Often, they were largely supported financially by the party or its members.

Most such papers were fiercely partisan. They made little, if any, attempt to report objectively on political affairs. Editors did not see their job as requiring them to present both sides of political issues, but rather to propagandize for one side or the other. In doing so, they made little distinction between facts and political opinion. The facts they did present were usually selected, and often distorted, in order to make a political point.

If this was true in even the largest cities of the East in the first part of the nineteenth century, it was even more true in the small towns of the western frontier. Most of the frontier papers were published virtually single-handed, by an editor-publisher who used the paper as a medium of personal political expression. The western editors had a reputation for personal eccentricities and for fierce partisanship in political matters, and both were reflected in the papers they turned out.

The political bias of these partisan papers was open and unrelenting. Almost every issue would feature glowing praise for one party or politicial position and bitter denunciation of all others. This bias was even more pronounced at election time. Candidates an editor approved of would receive column after column of attention. Opposing candidates were often not even mentioned. When they were, it was only to revile them.

Name-calling of the most vicious kind was commonplace. Political opponents were regularly libeled as "drunkards," "thieves" and worse, in the pages of the partisan press. Even presidents were vilified. Thomas Jefferson, for example, was labeled an "Infidel" by one paper, while others accused him of fathering several illegitimate children by a slave. Things got so bad that Jefferson, a longtime champion of freedom of the press, complained that his opponents "fill their newspapers with falsehoods, calumnies, and audacities." On another occasion, he wrote to a friend that "Advertisements contain the only truths to be relied on in a newspaper." Although Jefferson was speaking of the Federalist press, which was opposed to him, he might also have been speaking of the Democratic Republican papers that supported him. His own party's papers were every bit as vicious and libellous as those of his opponents.

The effects of this bias on the part of individual newspapers was offset by the fact that most cities, and even most small towns, had at least two newspapers. Each would represent a different party, and select, and sometimes distort, its facts accordingly. While these papers did not represent all possible political views, they usually represented those that were most widely held in their communities. Readers at least had a choice, and, given the obvious bias of such papers, it is likely that most readers took them all with a suitable grain of salt.

The Popular Press

Richard Steele published the first issue of his famous paper, *The Tatler*, in London in 1709. In that first issue, he announced that his new paper was "principally intended for the Use of Politick Persons, who are so publick-spirited as to neglect their own Affaires to look into Transactions of State." He went on to describe the purpose of his new paper this way: "[T]hese Gentlemen, for the most part, being Persons of strong Zeal and weak Intellects, It is both a Charitable and Necessary Work to offer something, whereby [they] may be instructed, after their reading, WHAT TO THINK."

Steele was speaking with his tongue in his cheek, of course, but the papers of the eighteenth and early nineteenth centuries *were* principally intended for the kind of readers he described. They were men who were interested in politics, and who were sufficiently well off economically to afford to spend time on such affairs. Women, who could not vote, were assumed to be uninterested in such things, while the poor were too busy working to put food on the table to concern themselves with politics. The poor, in any case, were considered politically irrelevant. "Transactions of State" were the business of men of property. And many of the papers of the time *did* attempt to influence what their readers thought. All this was as true, if not more so, in America as it was in England—at least at first.

Until the 1830s, American newspapers were written almost exclusively for well-to-do readers. They were largely devoted to politics or commercial advertising, both of which were primarily of interest to the propertied classes. What is more, the early papers were too expensive for most ordinary citizens to afford. They were sold by subscription, and a year's subscription to a big-city daily would cost the average laborer a full week's wages. As a result, they tended to reflect, and rein-force, the views of the wealthier elements of American society.

The year 1833, however, saw the birth of the penny paper—a newspaper that could be purchased one copy at a time instead of by subscription, and for only 1 cent an issue. Suddenly almost everyone who was literate—and more and more Americans were becoming literate all the time—could afford to read a newspaper. For the first time, America had a truly popular press—a press that appealed to ordinary members of the public, and not just to the social and political elite. It was this press that would dominate American journalism throughout the rest of the nineteenth century.

The lower price, of course, meant that more copies had to be sold in order to make a paper profitable. This meant that it was suddenly more important for news-papers to attract large numbers of readers. Partly be-cause of this new need, the nature of American news-papers changed rapidly in the 1830s and 1840s, as editors scrambled to find new ways to attract readers.

Perhaps the most dramatic of the changes was a new emphasis on news reporting: that is, on the timely reporting of current events. In the days when papers had only come out every week or two, current news, as such, had not been considered of great importance. But now, editors discovered that readers enjoyed get-ting news—news of political events, news of wars and revolutions, news of scientific discoveries, news of just about anything at all. And the faster the better. The first paper to appear with the news of an important event would sell more copies that day. The result was a fierce competition among newspapers to get the news, and to get it first.

One side effect of this competition for news was the introduction of crime reports. Crime, particularly petty crime, had not been considered either important enough or interesting enough to be printed in the newspapers before. After all, in the view of the prosperous readers of the early papers, the lower classes were always robbing, assaulting and murdering each other. Upper-class readers could hardly be expected to interest themselves in the sordid details of such behavior. To them, crime was an unpleasant fact, but not a particularly significant one. The *New York Sun*, however, taking its lead from some popular English newspapers, discovered that crime news provided a kind of entertainment for the new readers of the popular press. The *Sun* began running brief daily reports about such previously unreported events as robberies, sexual assaults, wife beatings, arrests for public drunkenness, prostitution and the like. Readers loved them. They found the sins of their neighbors immensely enjoyable to read about. Before long, many other papers followed the *Sun*'s lead, and crime news became a regular staple of the American press.

Not all observers of the popular press applauded its influence on the public. The artist who drew this cartoon reflected the fear that such newspapers as the Police Gazette *could turn gentle ladies into hard-drinking, pipe-smoking readers of lurid crime stories.*

There were many other innovations in the popular press of the time. The new class of readers had a previously unsatisfied appetite for information about their social "betters." The penny papers rushed to feed this appetite by publishing social calendars, gossip and scandal concerning the members of the upper class. Readers also seemed to have an insatiable desire for news of disasters and freaks of nature such as two-headed babies and circus geeks who ate live snakes. Along with such sensational material, serialized novels and sentimental fiction, theatrical and literary reviews, and reports of travel to exotic lands all became staples of the popular press. And, since middle-class housewives were beginning to read the papers in large numbers, such homely features as recipes and household tips began to appear as well.

Moon-bats

In the competition for readers, accuracy often counted for little. Stories were routinely embellished out of all proportion. If they seemed likely to attract readers, it hardly mattered whether there was any truth to them or not. The attitude of many editors was expressed by James Gordon Bennett of the immensely popular *New York Herald* when he warned a young reporter to: "Remember, son, many a good story has been ruined by over-verification."

Sometimes, stories were made up entirely and designed specifically to attract the attention of the public. The most famous of all such stories, and the most successful ever to appear in the penny press, was published by the *New York Sun* in August of 1835. Claiming to be reprinting excerpts from the journal of a renowned British astronomer, Sir John Herschel, the paper announced the existence of manlike creatures on the moon.

The creatures, whom the author called "man-bats," were described as "four feet high," and "covered, except in the face, with short, glossy, copper-colored hair." They might almost have been mistaken for humans, except for their wings. These were "composed of a thin membrane, without hair," and "lay upon their backs from the top of their shoulders to the calves of their legs."

The "excerpts," which had actually been written by the paper's star reporter, Richard Adams Locke, were so clever that they were taken seriously not only by the public but by other newspapers, which reported the "discovery" as a genuine news story. The hoax fooled people from all classes of society, even many scientists themselves. Yale University sent a delegation of experts to the *Sun* to study the original (nonexistent) journal. The paper's circulation is said to have jumped from 15,000 to 65,000 in the course of a few weeks.

When the truth was revealed, it was clear that the *Sun* had been a knowing party to the hoax. The paper argued in print that the false stories had actually been a kind of public service, "diverting the public mind" from such serious issues as the mounting controversy over slavery. Instead of repenting its deception, the paper eventually printed several other hoaxes, including at least one written by the well-known writer Edgar Allen Poe.

What is most interesting about the revelation of this journalistic hoax is the public's reaction to it. They did not seem to care. If anything, they were more amused by the deception than angered by it. The *Sun*'s circulation remained the highest of any daily in the country, and Locke kept his reputation as one of the country's

*The famous cartoonist Thomas Nast satirized
the "moon-bat" hoax in this cartoon
depicting the ancient Greek philosopher Diogenes
searching among the popular newspapers of the
day in his legendary quest for an "honest man."*

leading journalists. This reaction suggests at least two things about the relationship between the press and the public in nineteenth-century America. First, the public knew it could not expect a high standard of accuracy from its newspapers; second, it wanted the papers anyway, whether it could rely on them to tell the truth or not.

This surprising tolerance did not necessarily mean that readers didn't care whether or not the papers told the truth. If asked, they almost certainly would have said they preferred truthful information from the press. Still, few if any readers deserted the *Sun* after the hoax was revealed, even though there were several other newspapers in New York for indignant readers to turn to. What all this may really mean is that people had come to look to the popular press for more than news. They had come to look to it for entertainment. As long as the papers were entertaining enough, much of the reading public was willing to accept them. And fiction was sometimes even more entertaining than truth.

The Political Effect of
the Popular Press
In some ways the popular press was less single-mindedly political than the early press had been. While many editors expressed strong social and political views, some of them maintained political independence. They were not tied to the views, or to the financial support, of a particular party or faction, the way so many of their predecessors had been. What is more, in their effort to attract larger numbers of readers, they tended to devote less space to partisan political matters and more to other kinds of news and features.

In at least one way, however, the political influence of the popular press was even greater than that of the earlier papers had been. It was much more wide-spread. The popular press reached many more read-ers. At the turn of the century, the largest circulation of any newspaper in the country was around 4,000. At the height of the "moon-bat" hoax, the circulation of the *Sun* reached 65,000. By 1860, the daily *New York Herald* had a circulation of over 75,000, while the weekly *New York Ledger* had 400,000! And both the numbers of newspapers and their average circulations continued to climb throughout the rest of the century.

The bulk of these readers were not the "Politick Persons" the early newspapers had been written for. They could not afford to "neglect their own affairs to look into Transactions of State." They were mostly small tradesmen and laborers, people who worked for a liv-ing, and worked hard, and who received very little in return. Perhaps partly because of this, many of the penny papers were reformist in their politics. They supported measures designed to restrict the power of the wealthy, and to promote the interests of the mid-dle class, the poor and the near poor who made up the majority of their readers.

This is not to imply that the editors and publishers who ran these papers were necessarily insincere. At least two of the most prominent editors of the nine-teenth century were noted for the fierceness of their commitment to reformist causes. Their views bordered on what today would be considered radical. These were Horace Greeley of the *New York Tribune* and Edward Wyllis Scripps, the founder of the first great American newspaper chain. Greeley used his newspaper to ar-gue for the rights of workers to form labor unions (he was the president of a printers' union himself), for So-cialism, and for the abolition not only of slavery but of the death penalty, among many other political causes.

Reformist editor Horace Greeley supported many liberal causes, among them workers' rights and the abolition of slavery.

Scripps, like Greeley, was a champion of the poor. He believed that most of the American press was controlled by rich capitalists, who made sure that the "great mass of people were kept ignorant." He was determined that his papers should give the people the information they needed to "vote and in all ways act in the best way to protect themselves from the brutal force and chicanery of the ruling and employing class." His journalistic philosophy was a simple one. "I have only one principle," he wrote, "and that is represented by an effort to make it harder for the rich to grow richer and easier for the poor to keep from growing poorer." Scripps's paper did not only speak *to* the poor and the near poor, "the large majority . . . who are not so rich in worldly goods and native intelligence as to make them equal, man for man, in the struggle with the wealthier and more intellectual class." It spoke *for* them.

Whatever else the penny papers of the nineteenth century accomplished, they certainly helped make the public better informed than ever before. Although some of the information they printed was unreliable, much of it was accurate. And the readers of the penny press were exposed to more news and information of both kinds than their parents and grandparents had ever been. As the famous preacher and newspaper editor Henry Ward Beecher expressed it: "Newspapers are the schoolmasters of the common people." They were also an important democratizing force. They helped to bring that "large majority" who were their readers into the political process more fully than they had ever been involved before. What is more, the popular press helped to set the tone for the new nation's development. When Horace Greeley advised "Go West, young man, go West," he was not only reflecting the great movement westward across the continent, he was encouraging it.

By the end of the nineteenth century, the American press had undergone a long transformation. It had also founded several new traditions. The newspaper had become a medium of popular instruction and entertainment. The definition of "news" had been broadened to include more than commercial announcements and political arguments. And, on the news pages at least, some elements of the press had begun to make serious efforts toward objectivity.

By 1896, the new publisher of the *New York Times* newspaper could declare that his paper's job would be, "To give the news impartially, without fear or favor, regardless of party, sect, or interest involved; to make the columns of the *New York Times* a forum for the consideration of all public questions of public importance, and, to that end, to invite intelligent discussion from all shades of opinion."

When Thomas Jefferson first suggested that the country might be better off without a government than without newspapers—*if* every man could read the papers—that seemed like an impossible dream. Only a small proportion of the population could read in Jefferson's day. But the popularity and large circulations of the popular newspapers of the nineteenth century seemed to be bringing his dream very close to reality.

3

Rebels with a Cause—
The Radical Press

. . . I do not wish to
think, or speak or write
with moderation. . . .
I will not equivocate—
I will not excuse—I will
not retreat a single inch—
AND I WILL BE HEARD.

William Lloyd Garrison,
in the first issue of his
abolitionist newspaper,
The Liberator

I n this book we are dealing primarily with the mainstream press—the major newspapers, newsmagazines and the national radio and television networks. But there has always been another press in America, one which has been outside the established order, and critical of it.

As we have seen, the American press, like the United States of America itself, was born in revolution. Its oldest and proudest traditions involve spirited attacks on the established political order. James Franklin, John Peter Zenger and Thomas Paine are among the earliest heroes of the American press, and they all became heroes in the same way. Each used the power of the press as a weapon against the political establishment of his time. This radical tradition did not end with the revolution. There has been a radical press ever since, out on the fringes of journalism, railing against the accepted political order of the day and demanding fundamental change.

This radical press should not be confused with the independent mainstream press, which is also often critical of the government and its policies. The radical press is more fundamental in its opposition. Its hostility is directed at something deeper than a particular governmental policy or administration: sometimes at the political system itself, and often at the economic and social systems as well.

There have been several varieties of radical publications in America, espousing several different political views. Some have favored more government involvement in people's lives, some have called for no government at all. Some have based their political views on religious principles, some have been atheistic. Some have called for nonviolence, while others have called for armed revolution. But all the radical press has called for drastic change—change more fundamental than the public-at-large, or the mainstream press, was willing to consider seriously.

The radical press has never been broadly popular. Instead, it has spent most of its time "preaching to the converted," to those few radicals who already agree with it. Most of the time the majority of people hardly notice the radical press, much less fall under its influence.

But, from time to time, elements of the radical press have managed to attract the attention of the public-at-large. In a few cases, they have done more. They have helped to change the public's perception of important political and social issues. At such times, the radical press has been able to exert an influence far broader than its own small following would suggest.

The Abolitionists

Perhaps the most far-reaching example of the influence that has sometimes been exerted by the radical press was that of the abolitionist press which fought against slavery in the decades before the Civil War. Today, when slavery is universally recognized as an evil, it seems strange to think of the abolitionists as radicals, but that is what they were.

In the early nineteenth century, slavery was an accepted practice in half the United States. Many important people, including some religious leaders, supported it. Owning slaves was not a crime. Escaping from slavery was. The institution of slavery was enshrined in the laws of the Southern states. Worst of all, the Constitution was interpreted as protecting the states' "right" to have slavery, and requiring the federal courts to respect their laws. It was because of this that the prominent abolitionist William Lloyd Garrison called the Constitution "a covenant with death and an agreement with Hell."

But the abolitionists were not radical simply because they opposed slavery; many nonradical Americans disliked it as well. The abolitionists were radical because, for them, the slavery question was fundamental. It overrode all other political and moral concerns. They were willing to sacrifice everything—even the Union itself—in order to abolish it. And it seemed as if that sacrifice might be necessary.

To abolish slavery would mean shaking the foundation of the Constitution, overturning the social order of half the country and driving the economy of the South—perhaps of the entire nation—into financial collapse. Not many Americans, even among those who believed that slavery was morally evil, were willing to take such risks. The radical abolitionists were.

They made their case in every way they could. The clergy among them preached against slavery from the pulpit. Speakers traveled about the country, lecturing against the practice to anyone who would listen. Some wrote books. Many broke the law to help slaves escape. And at least one famous band of abolitionists, led by John Brown, turned to what today would be called terrorist activities to try to force abolition. But, most of all, the abolitionists turned to the press.

Those mainstream newspapers that opposed slavery were too moderate to satisfy the true abolitionists, so they founded newspapers of their own. The most famous of these were Garrison's *Liberator*, which he founded in Boston in 1831, and *The North Star*, edited by an escaped slave named Frederick Douglass, who was probably the finest writer of all the abolitionist ed-

*Frederick Douglass, himself a former slave, wrote
forcefully against the institution of slavery
in his famous abolitionist paper,* The North Star.

THE LIBERATOR

VOL. I.]   WILLIAM LLOYD GARRISON AND ISAAC KNAPP, PUBLISHERS.   **[NO**

BOSTON, MASSACHUSETTS.]   OUR COUNTRY IS THE WORLD—OUR COUNTRYMEN ARE MANKIND.   **[SATURDAY, APRIL 23,**

THE LIBERATOR
IS PUBLISHED WEEKLY
AT NO. 11, MERCHANTS' HALL.

WM. LLOYD GARRISON, EDITOR.

T E R M S.

☞ Two Dollars per annum, payable in advance.
☞ Agents allowed every sixth copy.
☞ No subscription will be received for a shorter period than six months.
☞ All letters and communications must be POST PAID.

A G E N T S.

CHARLES WHIPPLE, *Newburyport, Mass.*
JAMES E. ELLIS, *Providence, R. I.*
PHILIP A. BELL, *New-York City.*
JOSEPH CASSEY, *Philadelphia, Pa.*
HENRY OGDEN, *Newark, N. J.*
WILLIAM WATKINS, *Baltimore, Md.*

THE LIBERATOR.

not the plea, that emancipation is impracticable, the most impudent hypocrisy and the most glaring absurdity ever propounded for contemplation ?— Can any suppositious expediency, any dread of political disorder, or any private advantage, justify the prolongation of corruption, the enormity of which is unequalled, or repel the holy claim to its extinction? The system is so entirely corrupt, that it admits of no cure but by a TOTAL and IMMEDIATE abolition. For a gradual emancipation is a virtual recognition of the right, and establishes the rectitude of the practice. If it be just for one moment, it is hallowed for ever ; and it be inequitable, not a day should it be tolerated.'

two committee men and a constable interfered, and would not permit him to take his seat ! He was finally driven away, and the pew passed into other hands.

We purpose shortly to visit all our meeting-houses, and ascertain what places are provided for the accommodation of our colored people. A house dedicated to the worship of Almighty God, should be the last place for the exercise of despotic principles.— But here is the extract :

' With deep regret we have observed some articles in the columns of the " Liberator," of Boston, apparently from this city, in which its inhabitants are implicated ; and which we believe the editor of that publication will deem very injudicious, as well as unkind, when knowing the truth in the case. So far from wishing to deprive the colored population of an opportunity to worship God, by the co-operation of the friends of religion with that part of the inhabitants, a good and convenient house was erected a few years since ; clergymen of different denominations have often officiated, gratuitously, from Sabbath to Sabbath ; and when disappointed in the labors of a Minister, lay brethren have attended at their request, and made exertions to promote the prosperity of their congregation ; for many years a Sabbath School has been taught, composed entirely of colored children and adults ; in addition to this, if we mistake not, at their request the public school money is given them in proportion to the number of their children, and they thus have a day school of their own.

After such interest had been shown for that class of people, was it to be expected that an attack should be made upon the very persons who have shown such liberality ? This is indeed gratifying to

be elevated and improved in this country ; unanimous in opposing their instruction ; unanimous in exciting the prejudices of the people against them ; unanimous in apologising for the crime of slavery ; unanimous in conceding the right of the planters to hold their slaves in a limited bondage ; unanimous in denying the expediency of emancipation, unless the liberated slaves are sent to Liberia ; unanimous in their hollow pretence for colonizing, namely, to evangelize Africa ; unanimous in their *true motive* for the measure—a terror lest the blacks should rise to avenge their accumulated wrongs. It is a conspiracy to send the free people of color to Africa under a benevolent pretence, but really that the slaves may be held more securely in bondage.' It is a conspiracy based upon fear, oppression and falsehood, which draws its aliment from the prejudices of the people, which is sustained by duplicity, which is impotent in its design, which really upholds the slave system, which fascinates while it destroys, which endangers the safety and happiness of the country, which no precept of the bible can justify, which is implacable in its spirit, which should be annihilated at a blow.

These are our accusations ; and if we do not substantiate them, we are willing to be covered with reproach.

In attacking the principles, and exposing the evil tendency of the Society, we wish no one to understand us as saying, that all its friends are equally guilty, or actuated by the same motives. Nor let him suppose, that we exonerate any of them from

virtue. I doubt not this conviction will ultimately prevail in every community, where the obligations of religion and philanthropy are acknowledged ; though the process may be slow ; having to contend with much ignorance prejudice and error. This conviction, however, is but the first step towards a redress of sensible as the total abolition of slavery. Whenever established custom acquires a strong hold on the feelings of those who are habituated to its continuance, they know that its power in many cases is almost unconquerable ; and this is especially the case, when the gratification of pecuniary emolument, or worldly aggrandizement, is to those interested in its continuance. It becomes necessary for the attainment of this great and good object—the universal emancipation of our colored brethren—the complete overthrow of this abominable traffic in human flesh—to investigate the whole subject fairly and calmly ; to discuss it freely ; to ascertain, as far as possible, what are the best means and methods for the accomplishment of this great end. On this point, I find the greatest diversity of opinion. Men of equal talent, equal piety, and equal benevolence, take different and most opposite views of the whole subject. My own mind has been much perplexed, by hearing what seem to me very strong arguments on both sides of the question.

With regard to the main subject, universal emancipation, as I before remarked, I have no doubt that think it may, and it ought to be accomplished ; but with regard to the means of its accomplishment itors. But there were also many others throughout the Northern states. (Not surprisingly, abolitionist papers were banned in the South.)

It took courage to be an abolitionist editor. The state of Georgia offered a $5,000 reward for Garrison's arrest if he ever appeared there. Even in the North, he was not safe. In 1835, he was dragged though the streets of Boston by a mob. A year later, another abolitionist editor named Elijah P. Lovejoy was murdered by a mob in the offices of his own newspaper, the *Observer*, in Alton, Illinois.

Like most of the radical press, the abolitionist papers were read mostly by people who agreed with them. At least at first. But as time went on, the popular press began to quote, and even to reprint, some of what they said. In this way, they began to gain influence with the public-at-large. They used that influence to arouse disgust with slavery, and along with it, hostility against the South. This disgust and hostility helped to prepare the way for the Civil War.

This is not to say that the abolitionist editors can take credit for *causing* the Civil War. Indeed, many would not have wanted to, since they were pacifists. Nor did they convert the majority of the public, even in the North, to their beliefs. Most Northerners remained reluctant to risk the Union just in order to get rid of slavery.

But the abolitionist press did manage to convert many people to their cause, and to prepare the North for the possibility of war. At the same time, it helped to inflame Southern feeling against the North, which many Southerners identified with the radical stands of the abolitionist press. Perhaps most importantly of all, by focusing the dispute between North and South on the issue of slavery, it helped assure that, once the fight

began, the North would have to demand the freedom
of the slaves.

The Radical Left

Most of the radical press in America has been leftist.
That is, it has tended to see society in terms of a conflict of economic interests between the rich and the poor,
and in that conflict it has sided with the poor. As a
result it has tended to be hostile to traditional capitalism. Opposing the concentration of wealth in the hands
of a small number of individuals and corporations, it
has called for a greater government role in distributing
the wealth of the society more evenly throughout the
population. Much of it has been frankly Socialist, calling for an end to the private ownership of the nation's
natural resources and major economic institutions.

Still, not all the nonmainstream press is to the left
of the political center. In recent decades, particularly,
there has been an active conservative press in America,
led by such publications as the *National Review* and the
Conservative Digest. But this right-of-center press is not
radical in the sense that we are using the term in this
chapter. While it has called for significant changes in
the role of government in American society, it has continued to support most of the fundamental principles
on which that society and government are based. Some
truly radical rightist organizations, such as the American Nazi party, have had press outlets, but those organs have not had any significant effect on American
political affairs.

The leftist tendency of the radical press dates back
at least as far as the abolitionist press of the 1800s. Although the abolition of slavery was its first concern, it
was not its only one. Most abolitionist papers supported a range of other causes as well—causes that are

often identified with the political Left. These included various kinds of socialism, pacifism, labor unionism, prison reform and the granting of greater rights to racial minorities, the poor and women. Such prominent abolitionists as William Lloyd Garrison, the poet Ralph Waldo Emerson and the ex-slave Frederick Douglass were among the earliest male supporters of the women's rights movement. (At the same time, many of the early feminists were strong supporters of the cause of abolition.) Many of the more mainstream editors, like Horace Greeley, supported a range of causes that today would be considered leftist as well, although their papers were not generally regarded as part of the radical press.

Other papers and magazines, however, were more determinedly radical. These included such major Socialist newspapers as the *Milwaukee Leader* (published by Victor Berger, later a Socialist party congressman from Wisconsin) and the *New York Call*, as well as many smaller publications. Some of them consisted of little more than tirades against the "masters" and the "bloated capitalists," as they referred to employers and other businessmen.

The early twentieth century saw the birth of an independent freewheeling radical magazine called *The Masses*. It attacked American capitalism with a zestful combination of wit, indignation and high spirits. Although its circulation never reached as high as 20,000, its influence was greater than that of many larger, nonradical publications. This was due to the unusually high quality of *The Masses'* contributors. They included the magazine's editor, Max Eastman; the short story writer, Sherwood Anderson; the poet, Carl Sandburg; the Pulitzer Prize–winning novelist, Upton Sinclair; and the journalist, John Reed, who later died while reporting on—and participating in—the Russian Revolution, and became the only American to be buried in the Kremlin. All of them wrote for *The Masses* without pay, just to be a part of the magazine and the political, social and literary movements it represented.

Most other radical publications of the time were less exciting, as well as less significant. Perhaps the most notable among them was the *Daily Worker*, the official newspaper of the American Communist party. For decades, this dull, dogmatic publication served as a kind of political bible, spelling out the "Party line" for the Party's small but committed group of followers in the United States.

The Radical Sixties

The 1960s and early 1970s were a time of social unrest in the United States. The 1950s had been a conservative decade, both politically and culturally. In the 1960s, American politics, as well as American culture, moved to the left.

The country had not been so divided, so openly and in so many ways, since the Civil War. It was a decade in which hundreds of thousands of Americans demonstrated publicly against their own government, and openly broke the law to protest the government's policies.

The main issues dividing the country involved poverty and civil rights abuses at home, and the war in Vietnam. In the South, black Americans had been segregated and denied their rights as citizens ever since the end of Reconstruction in the 1870s. The poor of the nation, both black and white, had long been suffering all but unnoticed by most other Americans. In the mountains of Appalachia, and in the racial ghettos of the cities, as well as in many other places, the life expectancy of the poor was appallingly short; hunger was an accepted fact of life, and children grew up without the hope of a decent education, much less of a decent job.

Added to these racial and economic divisions, was a division of generations. The largest generation of young people in American history—the so-called baby boomers who had been born after World War II—were coming of age. For the first time in history there were more Americans under the age of twenty-five than over it.

This new generation was different in many ways from the generation that had come before it. It was the first generation to grow up with television and rock music, and the threat of nuclear war. It was also the first generation to experiment so broadly with a variety of mind-altering drugs. All these factors served to separate them from the ideals and values of their parents—moral, cultural and political—and to make them more radical. But perhaps the most radicalizing factor of all was the Vietnam War.

As American involvement in the war grew steadily, that involvement became more and more controversial. Many Americans strongly supported our participation, and some even wanted to see it increased. But others were confused by the war, and wondered why we should be involved at all. Still others were completely opposed to our involvement. This feeling was particularly widespread among the baby boomers—large numbers of whom were being drafted to fight in the war.

Many members of all these groups—the blacks, the poor, the rebellious younger generation and those opposed to the Vietnam war—expressed their discontent publicly. In the South, black activists, along with some white allies, protested the Jim Crow laws. In the impoverished racial ghettos of the North, riots broke out in desperate response to the terrible conditions there.

On college campuses, and in some big-city neighborhoods, whole groups of young people adopted a new life-style. They called themselves "hippies" and "flower children." Many of them used illegal drugs openly, defying the police to arrest them, and challenged authority in a variety of other ways as well.

Many young men publicly broke the law by burning their draft cards (identity cards they were required to carry to show that they were registered with the draft). Some were sent to jail, some fled to Canada and elsewhere where they would be safe from the reach of the Selective Service which enforced the draft.

All of these protests were at least partly political. They were ways of demanding political change. And many of the participants saw all these demands as interconnected. They saw themselves as part of a broad political movement, seeking radical change in American society. Not surprisingly, many of these new radicals did what American radicals had always done: they established their own publications to publicize their ideas.

It was an unusually easy time to found small magazines and newspapers. Recent technological developments made it possible to turn out thousands of copies almost instantaneously, at very little expense. New radical publications sprang up all over the country, especially on or near college campuses. They included the *Barb* (of Berkeley, California), the *East Village Other* (New York City), the *Open City* (Los Angeles) and the *Great Speckled Bird* (Atlanta). They ranged in size and quality from simple mimeographed sheets to a slick-covered, high-quality magazine named *Ramparts*.

Collectively, the new radical journalism came to be called by several names. Because the Establishment it opposed included the traditional news media, it was referred to as the "alternative press"; because it championed new social and cultural values, it was called the "counterculture" press; and, most colorfully, because of its revolutionary tone, it was given the title of the "underground press."

Some of the new publications were exclusively political in content. They consisted entirely of editorials espousing antiwar and anticapitalist causes, and news items that reflected badly on the government and the military. Several were frankly revolutionary. Some even called for violence against the established political order. At least one actually printed instructions for making homemade bombs to be used against government property. Others were earnestly pacifistic, opposing both the war in Vietnam and violence at home.

Others hardly mentioned political matters at all. They were completely devoted to questions of the new radical life-style. They printed articles describing the new psychedelic drugs and advising readers how to get the "best high." They praised the new music, and the "hip" experimental literature and drama of the time. They carried "personal" advertisements for people who wanted to engage in unusual living arrangements or sexual activities. Much of what appeared in them was written in the most raw and vulgar language imaginable—a deliberate attempt to defy traditional standards of journalistic good taste. Many of the new publications combined all these functions, mixing questions of radical politics and radical life-styles together.

Some of what was printed in these radical publications was journalistically irresponsible: unverified charges, often based on little more than an editor's drug-induced fantasies. But much of what was printed in the best of them, such as *Ramparts*, was accurate, and led even the mainstream press to raise serious questions about American government policy and the conduct of the war.

It is impossible to say just how many of these publications there were. In early 1968, the heyday of the underground press, it was estimated that there were between 150 and 200 of them. In the whole decade there were probably more than twice that number. It is equally difficult to determine how many people read them. The most conservative estimate of their combined readership was 330,000 (made by *The Wall Street Journal*), while an officer of a news service that supplied them with material estimated 4,600,000.

The majority of these readers were young, in their late teens or early twenties, and most were college students. It was precisely this group—informed and egged on by the underground press—that spearheaded the agitation for civil rights and against the Vietnam War which so changed American politics in the 1960s. Legal segregation was ended in the South; major new social programs were introduced to help the poor; public sentiment eventually moved against the war; and women's rights became an important national issue for the first time since the nineteenth century.

All of these changes are still having their effects on American society today. All of them, for good and bad, grew out of the turmoil of the 1960s and 1970s—a turmoil in which the underground press played a highly visible part. Like the abolitionist press a century earlier, the underground press did not *cause* the political movement of which it was a part. But it encouraged that movement, and helped to make it succeed.

4

Bloody Shirts and Battle Flags—
The Press at War

Wars sell newspapers.

An American
newspaper editor

A s we have seen in earlier chapters, the Patriot press helped lay the foundation for the American Revolution and the abolitionist press helped prepare much of the nation for the Civil War. But these are not the only wars the press—or at least some elements of it—had a role in fomenting. In most cases, however, that role was a minor one. Many newspapers and commentators, for example, editorialized that the United States should join the Allies against Germany in World War I, but it wasn't until after Germany launched submarine attacks against neutral shipping that America actually went to war. Even more newspapers argued for American entry into the war against Hitler, but it was only the Japanese bombing of Pearl Harbor that finally prompted the United States to declare war on both Japan and her ally, Germany.

The extent to which the press contributed to American entry into those wars is arguable. Certainly the prompting of the prowar press had some influence on popular opinion, but there is no way to tell how much. At the same time, other elements of the press were pushing just as hard for America to stay neutral. Ultimately, most historians believe, there were important political, diplomatic, economic and military reasons for the United States to have entered those wars. It seems likely, then, that it would have done so whatever position the press had taken.

But in at least one case, many historians believe the press actually caused America not only to enter but to *start* a war. It did so by a practice known as "waving the bloody shirt." That is, by deliberately arousing public indignation against a potential enemy. As one writer explained the process in 1840, "It is by spreading the bloody shirt of some victim, and the humiliation of all, that the people are excited to take arms." That is what

certain important elements of the press did success-
fully in 1898.

In that year, María Cristina was the regent of Spain,
William McKinley was president of the United States
and William Randolph Hearst was the editor of the New
York *Journal*. Of the three of them, Hearst seems to have
had the most to do with bringing about war between
the United States and Spain.

As the year began, Spain was engaged in a contin-
uing struggle against a small group of guerrilla forces
in its island colony of Cuba, about ninety miles off the
coast of Florida. Meanwhile, in New York City, Hearst's
Journal was carrying on its own little war—a circulation
war with Joseph Pulitzer's New York *World*.

The two papers were competing fiercely to attract
readers. The unethical practices they used to do so included huge and often misleading headlines, printing
faked pictures and publishing sensational, but completely invented, news stories. Desperately searching
for new subjects to write about, both papers eventually
discovered the ongoing struggle in Cuba. As the papers described it, that struggle was a clear-cut case of
good versus evil, of a noble little neighbor battling for
its freedom against a large, cruel empire. Properly ex-
ploited, it was just the kind of story to arouse public
sympathy—and to attract readers.

In reality, things were grim enough in Cuba to
arouse anyone's sympathy. Taunted by the guerrilla
forces, the Spanish military had instituted a concentration camp system that kept virtually the entire rural
population of the island restricted to certain areas under armed guard. The military were sometimes cruel,
and the disease and hunger that haunted the camps
were even crueler.

But, bad as things were, they were not bad enough to satisfy the needs of Hearst and Pulitzer. They had to have ever more gruesome stories with which to lure readers. The papers began inflating minor incidents in Cuba into major ones on their front pages, all designed to incite hostility toward Spain. When the Spanish military forces failed to provide them with suitable atrocities to report, the editors had their reporters invent them instead.

The *Journal* and the *World* were not the only papers to join in the propaganda battle against Spain. Other papers across the country took part as well. But the two large New York papers were the main protagonists, and, of them, the *Journal* proved itself to be the true master of jingo journalism. ("Jingoism" is a kind of aggressive, chest-beating patriotism, one that tends to favor a chauvinistic, warlike foreign policy.)

At one point, when a young Cuban woman was imprisoned for attempting to assassinate the colony's military governor, Hearst launched a campaign in the *Journal* to pressure for her release. (And, of course, to increase the circulation of the *Journal*.) He published impassioned editorials detailing the cruel treatment she was supposedly receiving. These editorials were inflammatory in every way. They appealed as much to the racial prejudices of the readers as to their natural sympathy for a young woman in trouble. She was described as "the most beautiful girl on the island of Cuba," who had been imprisoned by a "lecherous . . . scoundrel," and thrown in among "the most depraved Negresses of Havana."

Hearst's efforts were successful, both in arousing public sympathy for the girl in the United States and in building up the circulation of his newspaper. Even when many other papers started following the story, it only pointed up the fact that the *Journal* had manufactured a heroine of truly national interest. Then, in an act of enormous daring—as well as enormous presumption—Hearst sent a reporter to Cuba to rescue the girl from prison. The reporter, Karl Decker, was successful not only in breaking her out of jail, but in smuggling her to the United States where Hearst himself presented her to President McKinley. By this time, Hearst, with some help from Pulitzer and other editors, had succeeded in setting American public opinion firmly against Spain in Cuba.

Furnishing a War
Hearst was not done. He knew a good thing when he saw it, and he was determined to keep using the Cuban situation for his own ends. His only real obstacle was that very little was actually happening in Cuba at that time. When Hearst sent the famous illustrator, Frederic Remington, to Cuba to draw pictures of the conflict there for the *Journal*, Remington could find few subjects. He is reported to have sent the following telegram to Hearst in New York:

> EVERYTHING IS QUIET. THERE IS NO TROUBLE HERE. THERE WILL BE NO WAR. I WISH TO RETURN.

His boss replied:

> PLEASE REMAIN. YOU FURNISH PICTURES. I WILL FURNISH WAR. HEARST.

And that is precisely what he did. María Cristina did not want war. President McKinley did not want war. But Hearst did. Not only would war spur his paper's circulation, it would further his expansionist political views. He, like many other Americans at that time, wanted the United States to assert itself as a world power and to found an empire of its own. Defeating Spain would establish the United States as the dominant military power in the Americas.

Then, on February 15, 1898, an event took place that was tailor-made for Hearst's purposes. The American battleship *Maine* blew up at its dock in the Havana harbor. The explosion killed 260 men and scuttled the ship. No one knew what or who had caused the explosion. But Hearst knew what use he could make of it. He could make a war.

A U.S. Navy inquiry concluded that the explosion had probably been caused by a mine, but that there was no way of telling who had put the mine there, or what had triggered it. The mine could have been set by Spain, or by Cuban rebels trying to cause trouble between the United States and Spain, or it could have been some kind of accident. A Spanish inquiry, meanwhile, concluded that the explosion had not been been caused by a mine at all, but by an accident involving American Navy munitions the ship had been carrying.

The *Journal*, however, insisted that the explosion had been caused by a "secret infernal machine," and that Spain had been responsible. That claim was, at best, a guess—but it was reported as a fact.

Hearst and his paper carried public opinion with them. The demand for war became a clamor, and McKinley asked Congress to declare war on Spain. Certainly the efforts of Hearst and the other prowar editors were not the only reasons the United States went to war with Spain. There were several real bones of contention between the two countries, and powerful interests in the United States who saw war with Spain as a step toward making the United States an imperialist power. Yet, without the rabble-rousing of the popular press, it is unlikely that war would have been declared. Most of the real issues given as reasons for war between the two countries could have been settled, to the United States' advantage, without military action.

In a sense, they were. Even before Congress acted, the Spanish government announced a cessation of hostilities in Cuba, and indicated that it was willing to give in on most of the issues involved. But it no longer mattered. American public opinion—virtually manufactured by Hearst, Pulitzer and a few others—was spoiling for a fight. War was declared on Spain.

From the point of view of Hearst and the rest of the expansionists, it was, as one of them described it, "a splendid little war." It lasted only a few months, the United States won several easy victories (which sold millions of papers) and firmly established itself as an important power. She even laid a claim as an imperial power. At the end of the war, Puerto Rico and Guam were ceded to the United States by Spain; and the Philippines, whose capital had been occupied by the American Navy *after* the armistice was signed, were "purchased" for the relatively small price of $20 million.

It was a particularly "splendid" war for Hearst himself. Besides playing a major role in starting the war, he had gone to Cuba to participate in it. A group of reporters, led by Hearst, actually captured a band of Spanish soldiers.

Many Americans, including most responsible journalists, deplored the tactics Hearst and Pulitzer had used to provoke the war with Spain. One journalist, Edwin Lawrence Godkin, wrote that "It is a crying shame that

863,956
WORLDS CIRCULATED YESTERDAY

The
"Circulation Books Open to All."
VOL. XXXVIII. NO. 13,419.

NEW YORK, THURSDAY, FEBRUARY 17, 1898.

World.
"Circulation Books Open to All."
PRICE

863,956
WORLDS CIRCULATED YESTERDAY

MAINE EXPLOSION CAUSED BY BOMB OR TORPEDO?

Capt. Sigsbee and Consul-General Lee Are in Doubt---The World Has Sent a Special Tug, With Submarine Divers, to Havana to Find Out---Lee Asks for an Immediate Court of Inquiry---Capt. Sigsbee's Suspicions.

CAPT. SIGSBEE, IN A SUPPRESSED DESPATCH TO THE STATE DEPARTMENT, SAYS THE ACCIDENT WAS MADE POSSIBLE BY AN ENEMY.

Dr. E. C. Pendleton, Just Arrived from Havana, Says He Overheard Talk There of a Plot to Blow Up the Ship---Capt. Zalinski, the Dynamite Expert, and Other Experts Report to The World that the Wreck Was Not Accidental---Washington Officials Ready for Vigorous Action if Spanish Responsibility Can Be Shown---Divers to Be Sent Down to Make Careful Examinations.

Joseph Pulitzer's newspaper, The World, *reports the sinking of the battleship* Maine, *suggesting in no uncertain terms that the explosion was an enemy action, the result of a "plot to blow up the ship." The result of such "jingo journalism" was a declaration of war against Spain.*

men should work such mischief simply in order to sell more papers."

Whatever else it was, splendid little war or crying shame, the Spanish-American War was one of the most dramatic examples of the power of the press in journalistic history.

Rallying 'Round the Flag

As a newspaper editor once claimed—and as the Spanish-American War demonstrated—"wars sell newspapers." Despite this fact, the press has never been unanimous in calling for American military action. Virtually every time there has been a chance that the United States might go to war, major elements of the press have argued against it. And yet, once the United States has actually gone to war, the majority of the mainstream press has tended to support the war effort, no matter what position the individual news organizations took beforehand.

Most often, criticism of the government is muted. While some criticism of military strategy might be voiced, little if any criticism of the American troops appears. They are described in terms of their "courage" and "valor," while the enemy troops are spoken of in terms of their "brutality" and "cowardice." American military victories are regularly reported in extravagant and overstated terms, while American defeats are downplayed. When defeats are so significant that they cannot be downplayed, they are portrayed as the result of overwhelming numbers on the part of the enemy, or of some sort of enemy trickery. Rarely, if ever, are they portrayed as resulting from American weakness or incompetence. Accounts of terrible atrocities committed by the other side help to inflame public anger against the enemy.

Newspaper headlines announce the bombing of Pearl Harbor, heralding an era when both press and public opinion rallied to support the war effort.

In essence, many news organizations become willing propaganda tools of the government. There are several reasons for this voluntary surrender of press independence. Some of those reasons are subjective. They have to do with the personal feelings of the individuals who make up the American press. Journalists are, as a group, as patriotic as most other Americans. If there is a bias in their reporting of wars in which America is involved, it is partly the inevitable bias of citizens in favor of their own country.

What is more, the war correspondents who do the actual reporting are ordinary human beings. They respond to what they see and hear, and to the people they meet. They spend a lot of time living with American troops, both on and off the battlefield. They share their discomfort and their dangers. They become their friends. They watch them fight, and suffer, and sometimes die. It is not surprising, then, that they tend to portray them in favorable terms.

Then, too, the American press tends to reflect the views of the American public. This is as true in time of war as it is in time of peace. A country at war usually "rallies 'round the flag." When family members and friends are risking their lives on foreign battlefields, most people do not want their nation's actions questioned, much less criticized. Much of the press is inclined to respond to this natural desire on the part of the public by giving the public what it wants.

But not all of the bias so often detectable in war news reporting is traceable to the attitudes of the press. Much of it is due to deliberate manipulation by the government and the military. The press, after all, can only publish what it can find out.

If the press tends to overreport news of American

victories, and to underreport news of American defeats, that may have to do with its access to information about them. There are limited numbers of war correspondents accredited to the American military. They could not be everywhere, even if they were allowed to be. And they are not allowed to be. It is usually much easier for reporters to get information about American victories than about American defeats.

Because lives—and perhaps the security of the nation—are at stake in wartime, ordinary standards of freedom of the press are made subordinate to the war effort. Despite serious questions about the constitutionality of the practice, the military is given the power to censor, to forbid the press to publish certain kinds of information.

But, even when censorship as such is not employed, the military can control much of the flow of information to the press. This is because the press has to rely on the military itself for much of its information. The information the military provides is often neither complete nor reliable. Necessarily, some information is withheld for security reasons. But some is withheld for public relations reasons as well.

Recent years have seen some of the most drastic measures yet taken by the military to withhold information from the press. Ever since the Civil War, it has been the practice of the military to allow war correspondents to accompany American forces into combat. But in at least two recent military actions—the United States' invasion of the Caribbean island of Grenada and its bombing attack on Tripoli, Libya—the press was not allowed to go along.

At times, military spokespersons have done more than merely withhold information from the press. They have deliberately fed reporters false information in order to deceive the public. As a United States senator pointed out nearly seventy years ago: "The first casualty when war comes is the truth."

5

Sounding Retreat—
The War in Vietnam

There gets to be
a point when the
question is, "Whose
side are you on?"

*American Secretary
of State Dean Rusk,
speaking to reporters
during the Vietnam War*

A lthough the majority of the mainstream press has tended to rally 'round the battle flag in times of war, there have been many exceptions. As early as the War of 1812, there were some newspapers that editorialized against the war effort. Several Federalist papers argued that the dispute with Britain was unnecessary and not worth the cost in money, much less in lives. Their stand was predictably unpopular. In one instance, a mob attacked the home of a Federalist editor, and a bloody battle was fought. Several people were killed, among them J. M. Lingan, who had been a general in the Revolutionary War, who died defending the editor's house.

During the Civil War, several Northern papers remained proslavery. At least four of them were denied the use of the U.S. mails because of their support of the South.

In the case of the war in Vietnam, some observers believe that negative reporting by the press helped to force the withdrawal of American troops. The press's role in that war was extremely controversial. (Technically, the United States was not at war in Vietnam. Congress never formally declared war on anyone. It did, however, authorize American military action in Southeast Asia in the Gulf of Tonkin Resolution of 1964.)

The controversy over the press coverage of the war centers around three aspects of it: the treatment given the opposition to the war here in the United States, the television coverage of the war itself and the publication of the so-called Pentagon Papers.

More than most other twentieth-century wars, the conflict in Vietnam aroused widespread opposition at home, and not just among the radical elements dealt with in the previous chapter. Partly this had to do with the draft and partly with confusion on the part of many

Americans about why the United States was involved at all. Tens of thousands of young men were being forced to fight a war they could not understand the purpose of. Others who examined the situation in Southeast Asia concluded that the United States was fighting to prop up a corrupt government against a popular uprising. Many prominent Americans—from the well-known actress Jane Fonda to the renowned "baby doctor" Dr. Benjamin Spock—spoke out against the war. There were large public demonstrations against the American involvement. Many young people burned their draft cards and committed other forms of civil disobedience to protest against it. Eventually voices were raised in the House and Senate in opposition to the war.

In the early days of the war, the antiwar critics were largely ignored by the mainstream press. They were dismissed as radicals and malcontents. But as more and more well-known people began to protest the war, and as more and more ordinary citizens began to question it, the news media began to give more attention to the critics. When demonstrations were held outside the Democratic party's National Convention in Chicago in 1968, television covered them extensively. When the police moved in on the demonstrators, beating several of them, some journalists openly criticized the police. Many supporters of the war felt that the press was too

This reporter was among the people beaten by police during demonstrations at the Democratic National Convention in 1968.

friendly to the critics, presented them too favorably and thereby helped them undermine the public's support of the American war effort.

Controversy also centered around the heavy coverage of the war by television. Every night, viewers of the national network news programs saw scenes from Vietnam: American troops in battle; Vietnamese women and children being attacked from the air; the execution of prisoners; and American soldiers, dead and dying. Americans regularly witnessed such terrible sights within days, or even hours, of their taking place. This had never happened before.

People became so used to watching the war on their home television sets that one television critic dubbed Vietnam "the living-room war." Quite apart from any bias on the part of the press itself, many people believed that this extensive television coverage had an important effect on the American public's attitudes toward the war. Just what that effect was is still hotly debated.

Some critics believe that it tended to trivialize the war, to encourage people to see the war as a kind of ongoing television show. Others felt that the constant graphic reminders of the horrors of war produced revulsion in the public. It made people react emotionally. The more they saw of the war on television, the less they cared about the reasons for American involvement, and the more they wanted that involvement to end.

To this day, there are people who believe that the extensive television coverage shortened the war. They argue that it weakened the public's will to continue the fight and helped to bring on the American pullout. Others believe the opposite. They are convinced that television lengthened the war by desensitizing many

Americans to the realities of it. The violence in Vietnam became less real to people because it was mixed up with the make-believe violence so common on prime-time television. If television *did* have any effect on the length of the war, it could be argued that it must have helped to lengthen it. The American military involvement in Vietnam was the longest military action in American history, lasting from 1961 until 1972.

Throughout most of the early years of that involvement, press coverage of the war followed the typical pattern. Little serious criticism of America's conduct of the war reached the mainstream press. That press tended, as it usually does, to accept, and to publish, official reports of American military activities. The picture painted for the American public was that of a series of successful operations designed to help a popular South Vietnamese government fight off aggression by the Communist country of North Vietnam.

As the conflict dragged on for years, however, evidence mounted that the government of South Vietnam was both unpopular and corrupt. Much of this evidence began to appear in the press. Meanwhile, journalists were getting suspicious of what the military was telling them. Some elements of the press began to be quite outspoken in their own criticisms of the military's conduct of the war, and to suggest that the public was not being told the truth about what the United States was doing in Vietnam.

Then, in June of 1971, *The New York Times* newspaper began publishing a series of articles which revealed a wide range of deceptions practiced by the American government on its own people. They showed that the government, including the military, had systematically hidden the extent of American involvement in the war from the very beginning.

The Times articles were based on what came to be known as the Pentagon Papers—a forty-seven-volume study of American activities in Vietnam which had been commissioned by the Pentagon itself. The study was classified Top Secret, but it had been leaked, or secretly given, to the newspaper by someone who had worked on the study and who wanted the truth to be known.

The government got an injunction ordering *The Times* to stop publishing the articles, but the Supreme Court struck down the injunction. The constitutional protection of freedom of the press, the Court ruled, took precedence over the government's desire to keep the papers' contents secret. (Two people the government accused of leaking the papers were eventually indicted for releasing them. Their cases were thrown out of court, however, when it was shown that the government had violated their rights in making its case against them.)

Although relatively few people read the full forty-seven volumes of the Pentagon Papers, many people read excerpts. Publication of the Pentagon Papers was devastating to many Americans' confidence in their government. And it had a significant impact on the public's perceptions about the war as well.

There is no way to measure the actual effect of the press coverage on the public's attitude toward the war in Vietnam. But President Lyndon Johnson paid an ironic tribute to still another role the press played in the war—its role as a reflector as well as a leader of public opinion. Late in Johnson's presidency, newsman, Walter Cronkite, went to Vietnam. He then gave a famous report on television saying that people had been misled about what was going on there. Far from succeeding, he suggested, the American effort there was in serious trouble. Hearing Cronkite speak, Johnson is reported to have turned to a friend in despair. "If we've lost Cronkite," he said, "we've lost the country."

Johnson's comment has been interpreted in two ways. Some people believe he meant that Cronkite was such an accurate reflector of national public opinion that his new opposition to the war was an indication that the public had turned against it as well. Cronkite was neither a sensation-seeking reporter, nor an anti-Johnson radical. He was regarded as a moderate, and as a careful and fair journalist. If the president's, and the military's, claims about the war were no longer credible to Walter Cronkite, they would no longer be credible to the mass of the American public either.

Others believe that Johnson's comment was a direct, if grudging, tribute to Cronkite's and the press's, influence on public opinion. Cronkite was the most respected, and the most watched, television journalist of the time. His critical report would not only be *seen* by tens of millions of people, it would be *believed*. Many viewers who discounted the criticisms of the war voiced by others whom they regarded as biased or radical would accept Cronkite's. In the atmosphere of the time, with much of the public troubled and confused about the war, Cronkite's attitude, the president believed, was enough to swing national opinion against the war. Whether Johnson was correct in his belief or not, the fact is that the war became increasingly unpopular. Johnson announced that he would not run for a second term, and Richard Nixon, who campaigned claiming that he had a "secret plan" to end the war, won the presidency in the next election.

Certainly the press cannot be given the credit, or the blame, for all of this. But many politicians, journalists and historians agree that the press in general had a great effect on public opinion about the Vietnam War.

The unpopular war in Vietnam proved the downfall of President Lyndon B. Johnson, whom the press widely criticized for escalating the fighting.

Critics of the war blame the press for so long accepting uncritically the government claims about what was happening in the war; supporters of the war still blame the press for what they feel was its undermining of the war effort by negative coverage of the military and positive coverage of the opposition to the war here at home. Ironically, then, the press has been blamed not only for prolonging the war with biased, prowar coverage, but also for ending it, with biased, antiwar coverage.

Although the press was not primarily responsible for either prolonging the war or ending it, critics on both sides have a point. Early on, the press coverage acted to support the war. Most of the press did report uncritically what amounted to government propaganda. Later on, however, press revelations of mismanagement and deception by the government and the military did much to turn public sentiment against the war.

6

Presidents and the Press

Political leaders,
by their very nature,
want to manipulate the
press to their agenda.

Michael Robinson

In many countries, the press is an official agency of the government. Its job is to act as a propagandist for the government, to present it to the people in a good light and to defend it from its critics. Even worse, there is little or no independent press to balance this progovernment one. Because of this, the flow of political information to the people is strictly controlled by the government. This is the case, for example, in the Soviet Union and throughout much of the Third World. In several other countries, even those with a substantial nongovernment press, government censorship is the rule rather than the exception.

In the United States, we have no official press. There *is* a Government Printing Office which publishes government documents, and there are people in various government agencies whose job is to handle public relations. But the news media, as such, are promised independence from the government by the Constitution.

Early in our history, however, there were attempts to set up something like an official—or at least a semiofficial—government press. President Thomas Jefferson, for example, established close ties with a newspaper, the *National Intelligencer,* and used it as a forum for his administration's point of view.

Of all the early presidents, however, it was Andrew Jackson who proved to be the most determined and skillful at manipulating the press for his own ends. This is not to say that Jackson obtained anything like unanimous support from the press. He never even received the support of a majority of the nation's newspapers. But he was extremely good at using the power of his office to marshal the support he needed.

In those days, newspapers were also printing offices, and Jackson made sure that papers friendly to him received a great many government printing jobs to do, while those that opposed him got none. And, like some European monarchs, Jackson put scores of journalists on the federal payroll.

He was particularly friendly with the men who ran the *Washington Globe,* a paper that had been founded primarily to help him. He looked to them for help in formulating his political policies, and he worked closely with them in presenting those policies to the public. His reliance on them, and on certain other journalistic cronies, was so great that they came to be known as Jackson's Kitchen Cabinet. It was widely understood that they were his closest political advisers. Probably no other presidential administration in history was so close to, and intertwined with, a group of journalists.

If Jackson's relationship with his Kitchen Cabinet was the closest any president has ever had with journalists, John Tyler's (1841–45) was probably the most extensive. He attempted to establish with papers all across the country the kind of relationship Jefferson and Jackson had had with the *National Intelligencer* and the *Globe.*

By the early twentieth century, newspapers were no longer the fiercely partisan propaganda sheets they had been a century before. Although they still took strong stands on their editorial pages, they made some effort to be objective when presenting the news itself, even the political news. Today, although many papers take editorial stands strongly supporting the policies of this or that president, newspaper editors and publishers no longer meet with presidents and plan strategies for promoting the president's programs. Most would consider such a thing highly unethical. Today, then, even the kind of semiofficial press represented by the papers mentioned above would seem drastically out of place, and even un-American, to most journalists, and to most readers as well.

Using Each Other

This is not to say that national administrations, as well as individual politicians, no longer make use of the press for their own ends. They do. Often with a kind of co-operation from the press itself.

Politicians and the press need each other. Politicians need the press for publicity: publicity for themselves and publicity for those ideas and programs that are important to them. The press, for its part, needs the politicians for information: particularly information about the government and what it is doing. These mutual needs establish a kind of partnership, however limited, between politicians and the press.

Politicians try to use the press to gain the public's attention, and to direct that attention where they want it to go. Sometimes they want this attention for themselves. They have to get elected, and for a candidate, publicity is vital. Sometimes, however, the politicians' desire for publicity is less personal than political. They may want to direct the public's attention to a particular political issue or social concern.

In any event, the politicians' main source of publicity is the press. It is largely through the press—printed and electronic—that the politician communicates with the people. It is through the press that the people hear what he or she has to say; and it is through the press that the people find out what the politician is doing, or not doing, on their behalf. The best crafted piece of legislation, the most stirring speech, the wisest policy is of little use to a politician if the people who elect him or her never hear of it.

In the modern world, politicians don't just need the

press to communicate with their constituents; they need it in order to communicate with their fellow politicians as well. In a real sense, much of the government of the country is conducted in the press.

Very few members of Congress have the time actually to listen to the debates on the floors of Congress. They are too busy participating in committee meetings, meeting with their constitutents, making public appearances, and so forth. What is more, with 100 senators and 435 members of the House of Representatives, personal contact between them all is virtually impossible. Often, the only solution for a congressperson with a point to make is the press. When a politician is "trying to get a majority of votes for a bill in Congress," Congressman David Obey of Wisconsin once explained, "what appears in the press every day is the best way to communicate with your colleagues."

There is also a negative side to the politicians' concern with publicity. As much as they desire *favorable* publicity, that is how much they dislike *un*favorable publicity. Put another way, politicians are very much aware that as much as the press can help them, it can hurt them as well.

For both positive and negative reasons, then, politicians do what they can to court to the press, to "manipulate the press to their agenda" as the well-known scholar and critic of the press Michael Robinson has put it.

The press, on the other hand, needs politicians for the information that they can provide. Information is the press's stock-in-trade, and politicians are some of the best sources for information about the vital subject of what our government is doing.

Because of this complex relationship between them, the two professions have developed procedures for dealing with each other: procedures for transferring information from the politicians to the press, and through the press to the public. What these procedures do is to set up certain rules under which information will be provided.

Some information is given publicly, as when a government official holds a news conference. Some is given privately, but "on the record," which means that the press is free to quote the source directly, and to give his or her name. Other information is given only "on background." This means that the press is free to use the information, but has to agree not to reveal the identity of the source. In such cases, the press often attributes the information to an anonymous source: "an administration spokesperson," for example, "an official of the Justice Department" or simply "a reliable source." Members of the public often assume that such terms indicate relatively low-level officials, but that is not always true. President Calvin Coolidge disliked being quoted and asked that reporters refer to him only as "a White House spokesman." Sometimes information is given entirely "off the record," which means that reporters are told about it only on condition that they agree not to use it at all.

Accepting these conditions, and others like them, is a common practice among American journalists. Reporters and editors accept them because they believe that doing so enables them to get—and to report—valuable information they might not be able to get in any other way. Other journalists refuse to accept them, however, on the grounds that they undermine the independence and integrity of the press. These journalists argue that such procedures allow the sources of information to dictate how the press will use that information. They take too much of the power of the press out of the hands of the press, and put it into the hands of the government officials and other politicians who provide the press with information. They are tools that politicians can and do use to manipulate the press, and to manage the news in their own interests.

Managing the News
Of all American politicians, none is in a better position to manage the news than the president. Whoever holds that office is uniquely able to influence, if not to control, what appears in the news media; and virtually all presidents, at least since Thomas Jefferson, have tried.

The president, whoever he (and someday she) may be, has virtually unlimited access to the news media. Even when the president does not specifically desire access, the media will be clamoring to give it. Any major news event, national or international, sends the press rushing to the White House for comment.

Much of the coverage of the president is uncritical. Presidential speeches are reported directly in the newspapers, or broadcast live and uninterrupted on radio and television. Such coverage provides the president with a means of speaking directly to the people. Most observers would agree that in providing presidents this kind of forum, the press is performing an important public service. Some journalists, however, would argue that presidents do often take advantage of it, and of their position generally, to manipulate the press and to manage the news.

As the head of the executive branch of government, the president controls a huge amount of information, including the wide range of economic statistics regularly compiled by various federal agencies. Such statistics are very important as indications of what is happening in the national economy, and they are often key factors in political debate. A presidential administration can use such figures to its own political advantage by careful timing of their release to the press. Good economic news can be released on a "slow news day," when there is little important news to distract public attention. Bad economic news can be released on a day when there are several major news stories breaking all at once, and the economic statistics can be expected to have little impact. Shortly before an election, administrations can, and often do, release a flood of good news, hoping to convince the public that things are going well. Bad news, meanwhile, can be held back until the election is over.

Some administrations have been blatant in their use of such practices. Others, such as John Kennedy's, have had a policy against them. They've set regular schedules for the release of government statistics, and stuck to them.

Aside from his ability to control the flow of information, a president's greatest asset in dealing with the press is his own person. Because he is president, he is news. People want to know what he thinks and what he does. Therefore, access to him is a valuable commodity to the press. And, while he has virtually unlimited access to the press, he can strictly control the press's access to him.

Presidents can make themselves available, or *un-available*, to the press on their own terms. They can decide when and where to hold a press conference, to give a major speech or to grant an interview. And whenever they do, they can be reasonably sure that the press will cover them. At one point during the Carter administration, the national television networks turned down a presidential request to address the nation. They claimed that the president had nothing newsworthy to say. But this was a glaring exception to the networks' usual practice—both before and since—of granting presidents time for such addresses whenever it is asked for. In this way, presidents can use the press to speak to the people whenever they want to do so.

In much the same way, a president can shut off access to himself when he does not want to speak to the people, or when he does not want to be asked about some controversial public issue. Woodrow Wilson did essentially that for years, dating from shortly before America's entry into World War I. Although no president in recent times has gone for years without speaking at any length to the press, and the public would probably not tolerate it if one tried, some have refused to speak to the press for long periods of time. President Reagan, for example, has gone for months without holding a press conference.

But, even while refusing to talk to the press, a president still has ways to use the press to his own advantage. One of the most popular among modern presidents is what is called a "photo opportunity." This is a chance for newspaper photographers and television cameramen to take pictures of the president. All the president has to do is to notify the news media that he will be in a certain place at a certain time and the media will flock there to record the moment on film and videotape. On such occasions, the president can virtually assure himself press coverage, without having to talk to the press at all.

By controlling the circumstances of a photo opportunity, a president can make a kind of visual statement to the public, without having to explain or justify himself. A president whose health has been bad, for example, might arrange to be photographed playing tennis. In this way he can suggest to the public that his health has improved, whether or not it has, without having to say so, or to provide actual evidence. A photo opportunity can also be used to make political statements. A president might allow himself to be photographed shaking hands with a political candidate in order to help that candidate's campaign, or with a visiting foreign leader in order to demonstrate American support for the leader's country. Ronald Reagan has shown himself the master at using the photo opportunity to the greatest advantage.

Some presidents attempt to establish personal friendships with reporters and editors. They get to know them, meet their families, have them to dinner. They flatter them by asking their advice. In all these ways, they attempt to charm newspeople, to get them to like them and to be on their side.

Some presidents have had a natural affinity for newspeople, and newspeople for them. Several presidents have actually been journalists themselves. Warren G. Harding was a newspaper publisher as well as a politician, and he continued to own a paper during his term as president. Herbert Hoover had been a part owner of a newspaper himself. John F. Kennedy had once been a working reporter, as had his wife, Jacqueline. It was not surprising, then, that these presidents established personal relationships with individual newspeople. Nor is it surprising that they made efforts to use those friendships to their political advantage.

Other presidents, too, have attempted to use their personal powers of persuasion—backed by the authority of their office—on reporters and editors. Of all the modern presidents, Lyndon Johnson was probably the best known for using the force of his personality to influence individual newspeople. Johnson was a large man, and intensely physical. He would put a huge arm

Three U.S. presidents meet the press, with expressions that reflect their relations with reporters: John F. Kennedy, who enjoyed a comfortable rapport with the press corps; Lyndon B. Johnson, who did not hesitate to blast his critics; and Jimmy Carter, whose uneasy relationship with the press deteriorated during the Iranian hostage crisis.

around newsmen's shoulders and whisper in their ears. A reporter who wrote a story he liked might be invited to Johnson's Texas ranch, where the president himself sometimes drove reporters around in his own car.

If Johnson was known for rewarding reporters who pleased him with signs of friendship, he was also known for his anger with those who did not. He would call up editors in the middle of the night, waking them from sleep, and yell at them for daring to publish a story he objected to. Nor was he the only president to try to intimidate the press. Although Theodore Roosevelt generally got along well with the press, was friendly with many reporters and was supported by many newspapers, he was one of the touchiest of all our presidents. He once went so far as to sue a newspaper editor for saying that he was a drunkard; and, as president, he ordered the Justice Department to sue several journalists for criminal libel. Among those named in the suit was the famous publisher Joseph Pulitzer. It was the first time the government had done such a thing in more than a hundred years.

Presidents have sometimes tried to get reporters they disliked fired from their jobs by putting pressure on their editors. While no responsible editor would give in to such pressure, such presidential tactics have a chilling effect on reporters and editors alike.

Although newspeople try to remain unaffected, both by presidential praise and presidential intimidation, many will admit that it is hard to disregard the opinion of a president of the United States. It is also hard not be flattered by his attention.

Some presidents have deliberately misled the press— and through the press, the people. They have distorted, or even invented, "facts" and released them to the press as true. Conversely, they have hidden true information which they wanted to keep from the press and the public.

Presidential administrations often classify as "secret," on grounds of national security, information that would be politically embarrassing to them. When such information has reached the press anyway, presidents have contacted editors and asked that it not be printed. Sometimes such presidential requests have been honored, at other times they have not been.

All of these tactics, and many others, have been used by presidents to persuade, intimidate, cajole and otherwise influence the press. Opinions differ widely within the news media as to how successful they have been. Some newspeople discount them, while others believe they represent a real danger to the integrity and the credibility of the press.

However much the press may worry about presidents managing the news, few presidents would agree that the danger they represent to the press is as great as the danger the press represents to them. There has probably not been a president in the history of the country who has not felt himself ill-used—if not actually persecuted—by the press. None more so than Richard Nixon, whose downfall will be discussed in the next chapter.

7

Bringing Down a President

In America,
the President reigns
for four years, and
Journalism reigns
for ever and ever.

Oscar Wilde

I n the early 1970s, two young reporters, working for a single newspaper, exposed the greatest political scandal in American history and forced the resignation of a president. The press coverage of that scandal, commonly known as the "Watergate Affair," demonstrated some of the best and some of the worst aspects of the way the American press covers the presidency.

Perhaps more than any other president in history, Richard Nixon hated and feared the press. This was true despite the fact that he had shown himself skilled at manipulating the press, and that the press had often been helpful to him. Early in his career, he had used the press to gain publicity for his efforts to expose what he believed to be Communist influences in the American government. He was only a junior congressman from California at the time, but press coverage helped to make him a national figure. When he eventually won the Republican presidential nomination in 1960, and ran against John F. Kennedy, he received the endorsement of the majority of the nation's newspapers. Even so, he seems to have felt that the press was hostile to him and treated him unfairly.

He made his feelings clear in a 1962 press conference held after he lost an election for the governorship of California. He was bitter as he faced the reporters at that conference, and he told them sarcastically that now, because of his loss, they wouldn't have Richard Nixon "to kick around anymore."

His retirement from politics was temporary, however, and he was eventually elected president in 1968. But even as president, Nixon remained bitter and suspicious toward the press. Almost immediately, his administration launched a secret operation to tap the telephones of prominent Washington reporters, and of

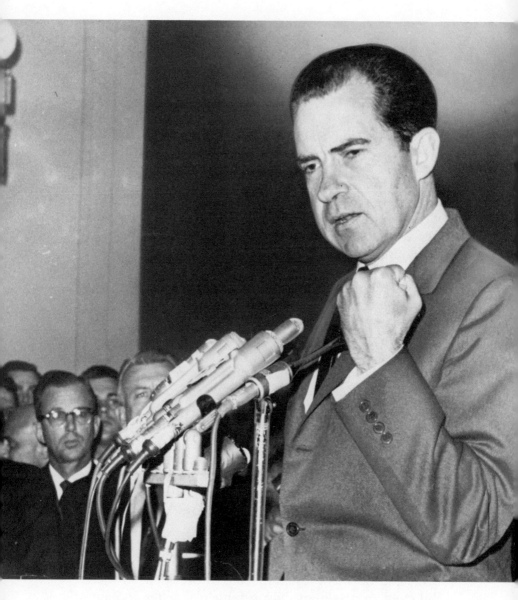

*Richard Nixon, at his famous "last press conference"
in 1962, was bitter toward the press for its
coverage of his California gubernatorial campaign.*

government officials he suspected of leaking information to them.

A "Third-Rate Burglary"
at the Watergate

At 2:30 in the morning of June 17, 1972, five burglars were caught in the offices of the Democratic National Committee in the Watergate Building in Washington, D.C. It was no ordinary burglary attempt. The men were carrying sophisticated and expensive electronics equipment—equipment they had been using to bug the Democrats' offices.

Within days, there were indications that the burglars had connections with the Nixon campaign. One of them was a recently retired CIA agent. Two of the others had the address and phone number of another ex-CIA agent in their address books. The captured ex-agent worked for the Committee to Re-Elect the President (known as CREEP, for short) which was Nixon's campaign committee. The agent whose address the burglars were carrying in their pockets worked in the White House.

Despite these sensational revelations, most of the news media quickly lost interest in the story. The White House press secretary shrugged off the incident as a "third-rate burglary," and most of the press seemed willing to accept it as that. The Democratic party chairman, Lawrence F. O'Brien, was not. He sued CREEP for $1 million damages, charging that it had bugged his office. Neither was the *Washington Post* newspaper, which assigned two young reporters, Carl Bernstein and Bob Woodward, to investigate the story.

It may seem strange that the *Post* would assign a pair of relatively inexperienced reporters to a story involving such serious charges against the political cam-

paign of the president of the United States. It may seem
even stranger that most of the rest of the national media gave even less attention to the story. Most major
news organizations gave it a very low priority, and most
veteran political reporters weren't really interested in
covering it.

There was, perhaps, a tendency of much of the media to give the president and his people the benefit of
the doubt. Some journalists, like many other Americans, simply could not believe that people so high up
in our government could have had anything to do with
such a shoddy affair. Others may have feared that to
play up the story would make it seem that Nixon was
right, that the press really did want to kick him around
after all.

This, however, only helps explain why most of the
media waited to give the story major attention until
more proof could be found linking the break-in to the
campaign. It does not explain why practically none of
the press, except for the *Post*, made any serious effort
to find that proof.

Some observers believe that the reason for the press's
failure has to do with the way it was accustomed to
covering political affairs. Investigative reporting forms
only a small proportion of American journalism at best
and is not seen as a major function of most political
reporters' jobs. For the most part, reporters were, and
are, accustomed to working "beats." That is, they have
certain more or less specific areas to cover, and certain
routine ways of covering them. In a political campaign,
for example, a reporter might be assigned to cover a
particular candidate. He or she would be expected to
follow the candidate, traveling with him or her, inter-
viewing the candidate, talking to the people running
the campaign, attending speeches and rallies to report

on what takes place at them, what is said and how the public reacts to the candidate. The investigation of the break-in at the Watergate was outside the usual beats of campaign reporting, and most of the veteran reporters apparently felt that they had enough to do without digging into a criminal investigation that might turn out to have nothing at all to do with the campaign.

For many critics of the press this general lack of interest was an example of one of the most serious failings of the American press: a lack of investigative zeal which seems to infect much of the news media, including most of the national news media. One result of this lack is a kind of excessive caution which leads the press to avoid controversial stories. Another is a failure of imagination, a tendency for the press to repeat itself, to fall into patterns, to cover the same stories in the same way, time after time.

The *Post*, however was an exception. Over the next several months, its reporters continued to investigate the apparent connections between the break-in at the Watergate and the Nixon campaign. Their investigation soon established that there were, at the least, serious problems within the president's campaign.

The Republican party, apparently unconcerned, renominated Nixon. The Democrats nominated Senator George McGovern. It was an unequal contest. The president was widely respected by the voters, while McGovern was viewed by many as too liberal for their taste. Voters who favored the American involvement in Vietnam appreciated such Nixon-ordered actions as the invasions of Cambodia and Laos. Even some voters who doubted the wisdom of that involvement were willing to believe that the president was trying to end the war as soon as possible. (A peace accord was signed the year after the election.) Meanwhile, Nixon made a diplomatically important visit to China which seemed to promise new hope for peace in the world.

McGovern, on the other hand, was viewed by many Americans as too "soft" on the war, and as the candidate of the leftists, the "hippies" and the misguided young. As if his candidacy was not in enough trouble, shortly after he was nominated the press revealed that his vice presidential candidate, Senator Thomas Eagleton of Missouri, had once been treated for emotional problems. McGovern initially supported his running mate, but finally had to encourage him to withdraw from the campaign. This seeming vacillation hurt McGovern's image even further. It seemed clear to most political experts that Nixon was a virtual shoo-in for reelection.

Nonetheless, the two young reporters continued their investigations, slowly gaining evidence that several members of the Nixon forces were engaged in criminal activities. They discovered there was a large slush fund of illegally donated money being used to disrupt the Democratic campaign and to spread lies about the Democratic candidates.

Much of their evidence came from people within the Nixon administration or campaign, people who were distressed by what was going on and wanted it stopped. Many of these people, however, were reluctant—or even frightened—to talk publicly. Many of the *Post's* stories, therefore, relied on anonymous sources.

One of the most important of these informants was a source within the executive branch of the government whom the reporters nicknamed "Deep Throat." He spoke to them on the deepest of deep backgrounds. Although at first he refused to volunteer any new information, he confirmed much that they had learned from other sources. Most importantly, he helped

Bob Woodward (left) and Carl Bernstein of the
Washington Post *began an investigation of a
burglary at the Democratic National Headquarters
in the Watergate complex that ended by exposing
America's most shocking political coverup.*

steer their investigation in the direction of the president of the United States.

From Victory to Disgrace

Nixon swept to victory with one of the largest electoral landslides in American history, but that didn't stop the *Post*. Its investigation continued, turning up increasing evidence of conspiracy among the burglars, CREEP and the White House.

The *Post*'s almost single-handed journalistic effort is generally credited with keeping interest in the Watergate affair alive. Eventually, in March of 1973, one of the defendants in the burglary case disclosed that the White House had conducted a massive effort to cover up the original crimes. A Senate committee was appointed under Senator Sam Ervin to hold hearings to investigate the charges of a cover-up.

If the *Post* had demonstrated the power of the printed press, the Senate hearings quickly demonstrated the power of television. The hearings were televised and millions of Americans watched spellbound, day after day, as witnesses testified under oath about the extensive corruption in the White House. It soon became clear that many government officials had been involved in crimes. John Dean, a lawyer who had advised Nixon during the alleged cover-up, testified that the president himself had been involved. Finally, another of the witnesses stunned everyone by revealing that the president had installed recording equipment in his own offices. Many of the president's presumably private conversations about Watergate had been recorded!

The recordings revealed that Dean had been telling the truth. President Nixon had been involved in covering up crimes. That was itself a serious crime—the crime of obstruction of justice. It was ironic. A scandal that had begun with an effort by Nixon's forces to bug his opponents had finally come to light because the president had bugged himself.

A committee of the House of Representatives drew up Articles of Impeachment against the president. They charged him with a variety of offenses. Among them were: interfering with the operations of the FBI, CIA and the Justice Department by ordering them to engage in crimes; misusing the Internal Revenue Service as a weapon against political opponents; and, of course, obstruction of justice. In the face of the impeachment proceedings, Nixon resigned.

As a result of the Watergate investigations, many of the closest friends, advisers and political associates of the president went to jail. Among them was the former attorney general of the United States, John Mitchell. Nixon might have gone to prison himself except that his successor, Gerald Ford, granted him a full pardon for any offenses he had committed while in office.

Many of Nixon's supporters still blame the press for "hounding" him from office. They claim that Nixon's offenses were minor, and that if the press hadn't disliked him, and played up the story, the whole Watergate affair would have been quickly forgotten. Nixon's hatred and fear of the press, they claim, had proved to be justified.

Defenders of the press respond that this is nonsense. Far from being too zealous in attacking the president, the press had been overly timid. Only the *Post*, it could be argued, pursued the Watergate story with any zeal at all. And the press could not be blamed for what it found out. It was not the press's fault that the president and the men around him, with his knowledge and support, had done what they had done. Nor was it the press's fault that Congress had moved to impeach him. The defenders argued, as Andrew Hamilton had argued centuries before, that the press hadn't brought the nation's leader into disgrace. His own abuse of power had done that. Even Nixon himself could not blame the press entirely for his disgrace. As he would later put it: "I handed them the sword—they twisted it with relish."

8

The Aftermath of Watergate

You [the press] are capricious
and unpredictable, you are
fearsome and you are feared
because there is never any
way to know whether this time
you will be fair and accurate
or whether you will not.

Karl Luedtke

Most Washington observers agree that the Watergate scandal left a backlash of distrust on the part of the press, as well as a large segment of the public, toward the presidency. Having been too ready to accept White House claims of innocence in that affair, much of the press determined to be more wary in the future. That legacy of suspicion would hang over Nixon's successors.

His immediate successor, Gerald Ford, was given a "honeymoon"—that is, a period of especially friendly treatment—by the press. It was, perhaps, even longer than most such honeymoons because there was a sense that the country had just gone through a crisis, and the public was looking for a period of calm and healing. Even so, there were serious questions raised by Ford's pardon of Nixon, and although criticism of the president was muted, there was still substantial distrust under the surface.

In the 1976 presidential campaign, President Ford was opposed by the Democrat, Jimmy Carter, a former governor of Georgia. The dark shadows of both Watergate and Vietnam hung over the election. Each of those events had damaged the people's faith in the honesty and competence of their leaders. Carter campaigned as a man who could heal the nation's wounds and restore the people's faith in government. Ford, meanwhile, presented himself as a president who was already in the process of doing just that.

The press was primed to be critical of both candidates. This was the first presidential campaign since the full scope of the Watergate scandal had been revealed, and reporters were determined not to let another such scandal slip by them. The honeymoon period with Ford was over, and they were, if anything, even more inclined to be suspicious of Jimmy Carter than of the president.

Carter's newness to national politics, his southern background and accent, and his claim to be a born-again Christian—all combined to make many longtime Washington reporters wary of him. Recalling that election, the veteran journalist Tom Wicker wrote that Carter was subjected to "the closest scrutiny and the most stringent standards" of "any presidential candidate of modern times. . . ."

Ford also came in for criticism, especially after he seemed to argue in a debate that Eastern Europe was not dominated by the Soviet Union. Journalists questioned whether he was really knowledgeable enough to make a good president. Some elements of the press treated Ford with an attitude approaching ridicule. Even his physical coordination was questioned. Despite the fact that Ford had been a varsity athlete, pictures of him bumping his head or tripping over rugs implied that he was exceptionally clumsy. Several publications quoted an old joke of Lyndon Johnson's who'd said that Ford "could not walk and chew gum at the same time." It isn't clear how much this treatment by the press hurt Ford's election chances. It may even actually have helped those chances with some voters by making the president seem more human and likable. Still, the press was tending to be more critical, and less respectful, than it had been of any recent president before Watergate.

Jimmy Carter won in a close election. Most political experts blamed Ford's pardon of Nixon for the president's defeat. Whatever the reason for his election, Jimmy Carter would receive some of the most negative press coverage of any president in modern history.

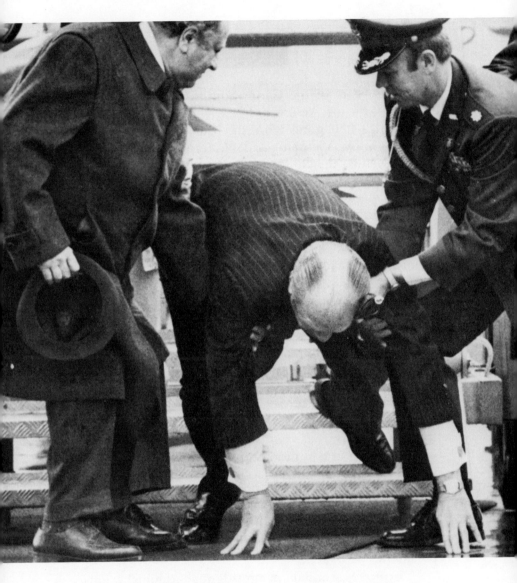

*Press coverage of Gerald Ford's clumsiness presented
a negative image of the president that some
said damaged his chances for reelection in 1976.*

President Jimmy Carter and
the Hostage Crisis
The four years of the Carter administration were un-
happy years for America. There was a general sense
that things had gone wrong in the country—a sense
generated by Vietnam and Watergate—and Jimmy
Carter seemed unable to do anything about it. Whether
because of his own economic policies, those of his predecessors, or factors outside any president's control,
the economy suffered severely. Unemployment was
high, and inflation soared. With the economy in deep
trouble, it was probably inevitable that Jimmy Carter
would be heavily criticized by the press. But many observers believe that he was subjected to unusually rough
treatment by the news media.

To be sure, the Carter administration handed the
press several swords of its own. There were scandals
involving both administration officials and Carter family members. Carter's friend and budget director, Bert
Lance, was accused of improper financial dealings in
his private banking transactions, and was forced to resign. Carter's brother Billy had a well-publicized drink-
ing problem, and was also accused of using his family
connection to obtain money from Arab oil interests. A
Carter assistant was even accused of taking cocaine at
a party. Although many of these accusations were later
shown to be groundless, they were widely repeated by
the press, and tended to produce an unfavorable public impression of the quality of the people around the
president.

Of course, scandals in presidential administrations
were nothing new. Even such popular administrations
as those of Harry Truman and Dwight Eisenhower had
had their share of them. But it seems that the press
was much readier to believe the worst of the people in

the Carter administration than it had been of those in previous administrations. The result was a sense on the part of the public that scandal was more pervasive in the Carter administration than in other administrations, a sense that was hard to justify from the objective facts. There was also a greater tendency to identify the president himself with the misdeeds—and possible misdeeds—of members of his administration than had usually been the case with Carter's predecessors.

Then, in 1979, events in the distant country of Iran grabbed the attention of the press, and the public, in a way that would severely damage the president's image as a competent handler of foreign policy. That November, hundreds of Iranian university students overran the American embassy in Teheran and took sixty-three Americans hostage.

The Iranian students made several demands in return for release of the American hostages—demands the United States was not prepared to meet. When it became clear that the students were acting with the support of the Iranian government, the hostage taking became more than a terrorist event. It became an international crisis between the United States and Iran.

It was probably inevitable that the "hostage crisis" would dominate the news for days. It was not inevitable, however, that it would come to dominate the news for the entire year that remained of the Carter administration. At first, unfortunately for him, the president seemed to encourage that domination. He announced that he would cancel many of his regular activities to concentrate on resolving the crisis in Iran.

It soon became apparent that a hostage crisis, like a war, sells newspapers. At least the one in Iran did. The news media emphasized and even sensationalized the crisis. Day after day, most major newspapers headlined the latest developments. And on days when there were no developments, they headlined that fact. One of the national television networks began its nightly news program by announcing that it was "Day Such and Such" of the hostage crisis. Another network inaugurated a special daily half-hour program in the late evening specifically to deal with the hostage crisis. (Eventually, the program would start dealing with other subjects as well. It became so popular that even after the crisis finally ended, the show—ABC's "Nightline"—would stay on the air.)

"America held hostage"—a phrase coined by the press—helped to form the public's perception of the crisis. It was no longer just a group of unfortunate American citizens who were being held captive, it was the honor of the country itself. The crisis, thanks at least partly to the press's intense focus on it, became a national obsession.

As the crisis dragged on into 1980, the president was increasingly blamed for his failure to resolve the crisis. Many editorials and commentaries suggested that the president was too weak and indecisive. Then in April, the United States launched a military mission to free the hostages. It had to be aborted when a helicopter crashed into an ammunition transport in the Iranian desert and eight American commandos were killed. Much of the press, which had been loudly attacking the president for not taking action, now rushed to blame him for being too reckless, and suggested that the failure of the military mission was, ultimately, his fault. It has to be understood that this approach was not inevitable. The press could have focused attention on the seeming incompetence of the military. Instead, it chose to focus on the responsibility of the president.

Nineteen eighty was a presidential election year, and

*Ted Koppel, moderator of ABC's "Nightline" which
began as a special nightly news program on the
Iranian hostage crisis. Inset: Iranian captors display
one of the hostages to the press. Television coverage
of the hostage crisis served as a constant reminder
of President Carter's failure to free the captives.*

the widespread perception of Carter as weak and bumbling in his handling of the hostage crisis had an extremely negative effect on his campaign. He lost the election to the former governor of California, Ronald Reagan, who portrayed himself as a "get tough" candidate. The Carter administration finally succeeded in negotiating the release of all the hostages, but only *after* the election. The hostages were only able to begin the process of returning home on the day Ronald Reagan was inaugurated—"Day 444" of the crisis.

It is quite possible that Jimmy Carter would have lost the 1980 election even if the press had not been so aggressive in publicizing the problems of his administration. The economy was in trouble. Many voters would have blamed the president for his handling of the Iranian crisis even if the press had not waved the bloody shirt so insistently. But the intensity of the press coverage—the daily reminders that the hostages were still being held and that the president was unable to free them—certainly built the crisis into more of an issue than it might have been.

If the press had handled the story with more restraint, the way it would later handle another hostage situation during the Reagan administration, the crisis might have vanished as a political problem for Carter long before the election. But instead, the press headlined the story for months, and then continued to run features on it right through the presidential election campaign. Just how much effect this had on the public's perception of the president is arguable. That it *had* an effect—and a negative one—is clear.

Ronald Reagan and
the "Teflon Presidency"
If Jimmy Carter was held to extremely "stringent standards" by the press, many observers believe that Ron-

ald Reagan was not. And yet, the Reagan administration handed the press at least as many swords as its two immediate predecessors had done.

If Gerald Ford made a serious error in stating that Eastern Europe was not under Soviet domination, Ronald Reagan made scores of similar errors. Time and again, the White House was forced to retract statements he'd made, or to "clarify" them to match with the facts. And yet, Reagan's image in the press, and with the public, did not suffer nearly as much as Ford's did over that single mistake.

Just as there were scandals in Jimmy Carter's administration and family, there were several scandals involving the people around Ronald Reagan. More officials of Reagan's administration were forced to resign than had been forced to resign under Carter. At least one was convicted of perjury—perjury which she claimed to have committed out of loyalty to the administration.

While inflation was alarmingly high under Jimmy Carter, the national budget deficit more than doubled under Ronald Reagan.

Several Americans were held hostage in Lebanon during Reagan's administration. Although there were fewer of them than had been held in Iran, they were kept prisoner for an even longer period of time. And yet, there were no suggestions in the press that America itself was being held hostage. For many months of the hostages' captivity, in fact, the press said so little about them that their families protested its silence. What is more, their plight had no effect on the presidential elections of 1984, in which Reagan won reelection by a landslide.

In October of 1983, 241 American marines whom the president had ordered into Lebanon to help keep the peace were killed by a truck bomb. Although the failure of the Iranian rescue mission and the deaths of eight American troops were treated as signs that Jimmy Carter was weak and reckless, the failure of the Lebanon peacekeeping mission and the deaths of 241 American troops had little effect on Ronald Reagan's reputation.

For some reason, none of these things seemed to harm President Reagan. Because of this, some journalists began to refer to him as the "Teflon president," after the nonstick cooking surface. Nothing—not errors of fact, not scandals in his administration, not even military disasters—seemed to "stick" to him. There were undoubtedly several reasons for this. The public certainly had an enormous amount of goodwill toward Reagan personally, for example, and inflation went down drastically during his years as president. Many other partial explanations could be offered as well. But one factor which must be noted is the significant difference in the press treatment of his administration's problems, when compared to the treatment given the problems of his recent predecessors.

It is not so much that the press set out to conceal Reagan's problems. Most of them were at least mentioned by the mainstream press, and some were even commented on in detail. But they were not dwelt on with the same insistence, the same intensity, as were similar problems in the Carter administration. What is more, there seemed to be less inclination to blame the president for such events as hostage situations, or economic problems, which were, at least arguably, beyond his control.

When asked about such differences, some journalists have claimed that the press was only following the public's lead. It was the *public* who had wanted to hear about the Carter family's problems, the *public* who were

Whether he is, in fact, the "Teflon President" or the "Great Communicator," Ronald Reagan has avoided some of his predecessors' problems with the press, even when the press has criticized his policies.

obsessed with Iran, the *public* who were angry with Jimmy Carter because of what they saw as his failures to solve these problems. When the news media did occasionally point out similar difficulties of Reagan's, the public was not nearly as concerned. It was this lack of public interest, much less anger—not any softening in the attitude of the press itself—that accounted for the differences in coverage between the Carter and Reagan administrations.

Other members of the press acknowledged another factor. They admitted that many members of the press felt that, in the backlash of Watergate, they had been too zealous in their treatment of the Carter administration. They had been too hostile and suspicious. They had attempted to hold the president personally responsible for too much. Particularly in regard to the hostage crisis, they had pushed too hard. In retrospect, there was probably little that any president could have done about it.

Having realized all this, these journalists admit, the press may have tried to make up for its overzealousness in covering Carter's administration by bending over backward to be more restrained in its coverage of Reagan's. The press backlash against the presidency had produced a backlash of its own.

9

In Search of Perspective—Questions and Controversies

To the press alone,
chequered as it is with
abuses, the world is
indebted for all the
triumphs which have
been gained by reason
and humanity over
error and oppression.

Thomas Jefferson

From the very beginning, as we have seen, the American press has involved itself in politics. The very first issue of the first colonial newspaper was banned because of its political views. The press helped to bring on the American Revolution; it helped to abolish slavery; it helped to elect presidents, and to bring them down; it played a role in starting at least one war, and in ending another.

Throughout our history, the press has been used as a forum for a variety of political views, both mainstream and radical. It has served as a pulpit from which editors and publishers have preached their political messages to the people. It has been a powerful propaganda tool for the government and for critics of government alike.

But even if the press had never deliberately involved itself in politics, it would still be politically controversial. That is because it is through the press that we receive most of the information on which we base our political decisions. As long as those decisions are controversial—which they always will be in a democracy—the press's role in providing that information will be controversial as well. In this final chapter we will briefly examine some of the questions and controversies surrounding that role today in the light of what has gone before.

Is the Press Biased?

Many people believe that the majority of journalists allow their own political beliefs to influence the way they cover the news; and that, since so many journalists share the same political beliefs, the public tends to get a slanted view of the world from the nation's press.

The critics are not primarily concerned about the editorial positions taken by the press. They are more concerned with the way they believe political bias slants the coverage of the news itself: both through the choice of what news to cover and through the way in which that news is reported.

What is news? To some extent, critics say, news is whatever the press says it is. There are uncountable numbers of events taking place in the world each day. Which of these are significant enough to be considered news—to be reported in the newspapers and on radio and television so that the public will find out about them—is decided by the people of the press.

Some events (presidential elections, major earthquakes, etc.) are clearly of great importance, and almost everyone would define them as news. But many other events are less obviously significant, and journalists must decide whether or not to report on them. Such decisions, critics believe, are inevitably affected by the political views of the journalists involved.

Take the case of a newspaper editor with room in his paper for only one local human interest story. His reporters provide him with two possibilities. One concerns a family living in poverty who are forced to sleep in the streets because their welfare payments have been cut off. The other concerns a young man, raised in poverty, who started a small business and quickly became a wealthy and respected businessman.

If the editor has a liberal bias, and believes the government ought to do more about urban poverty, he will probably choose the first story. He will feel that the public should be made aware of the plight of the city's poor, and that the story will help to inform them of it.

If, on the other hand, the editor has a conservative bias, and believes that welfare programs destroy character, he will probably choose the second story. He may feel that it presents a good example of how the poor should work to pull themselves out of poverty by using the free enterprise system. Whatever decision the editor makes, readers will learn of only one of the two situations—the suffering of a family in poverty, or the rapid success one man had in getting out of it—and not the other. And whichever story they read will have some small effect on their political perceptions.

The specific choice to use or not to use a particular story is probably not very important. No reader is likely to change his or her view of the value of welfare programs, or of free enterprise, as the result of a single story. But the sum of all such choices made by America's news media *is* very important. It is partly through such choices—made by tens of thousands of journalists across the country, day after day, and year after year— that the public's view of the world is formed.

The press can also slant the news by the way it handles those stories it does choose to cover. The same event can be covered in several different ways. The same crowd at a campaign rally might be described as "large and enthusiastic" by one reporter, and as "small and apathetic" by another. The first description implies, although it doesn't say so directly, that the campaign is going well, and that the candidate is popular with the voters. The second implies that the campaign is in trouble.

The same budget-cutting action by the governor of a state might be described in one headline as GOVERNOR REDUCES DEFICIT, and in another as GOVERNOR SLASHES AID TO THE ELDERLY POOR. Both headlines may be objectively accurate. The governor may have reduced the state's budget deficit by cutting a program designed to help elderly people living in poverty. And yet each headline gives readers a different political message. The first gives the impression of a moderate, responsible action by the governor, one that could mean lower taxes for the paper's readers. The second gives the impression of a drastic, even cruel, action, one that will hurt some of the most helpless and deserving members of society.

Such slanting of the news does not always result from a deliberate effort on the part of journalists. The hypothetical reporters and headline writers quoted above might each have been trying to be objective, to tell the truth as they saw it. But their perceptions of the events involved will necessarily be colored by their own beliefs and experience.

It is virtually impossible for a reporter to write a complicated news story without coloring it, to some extent, by choices of wording and emphasis. This means, of course, that it is virtually impossible for a reader to read a news story without his or her perceptions being colored as well.

Most critics of the press recognize the difficulties and acknowledge that a certain amount of bias is bound to be reflected in almost every news story. But many of them see a danger beyond the slanting of a particular story, or even of all the stories in a particular publication or broadcast. They believe that the majority of the nation's news media *shares the same bias*. This means as they see it, that the majority of the public is getting the same—politically distorted—view of the world from its news media.

Not all such critics agree about what that bias is, however. The most common charge made against the American press is that it is too liberal. They point to a poll that showed that more working reporters classified themselves as Democrats than as Republicans. (Many others classified themselves as independent.) But a number of other observers believe that the press is really biased toward a conservative point of view. They argue, as Edward Wyllis Scripps argued a century ago, that the major press organs of this country are owned and controlled by wealthy businesses and individuals who operate the press in their own interest.

Whatever the truth of these charges, one thing is clear from a historical perspective. However biased the press is today, and in whatever direction, it is much less biased than it used to be. Today, at least, most of the mainstream media attempt to be objective in their reporting of the news. How successful that attempt may be can be argued in any particular case, but the attempt is made. One hundred years ago, the sensational penny press made no serious effort to be politically objective. One hundred and fifty years ago, the partisan press made no effort at all.

Should the Press Be Balanced?
There is a widespread belief today that the press should provide balanced coverage of political affairs. This concept of balance implies that, when there are two or more candidates in an election or two or more sides to a political issue, the press should present each side equally.

For several years, the federal government actually demanded that radio and television stations and networks provide such balanced coverage. It could not make the same demand on the printed press because of the First Amendment. It argued, however, that the broadcast media were different. They were subject to government (public) regulation because they use the airwaves, which "belong" to the public. In recent years, as government regulation has fallen out of favor in many areas, the federal requirement for balanced news coverage has been weakened.

Still, whether required to or not, many journalists

believe that it is their obligation to provide such a balance. They see newspapers and radio and television stations as forums for political information and debate. Except for the single editorial page, or the brief editorial commentary some broadcast stations carry, they believe that the forums should remain neutral. And the only way to do this is to make sure that all sides of political issues are given roughly equal treatment. In practice, however, only a few sides of any issue are dealt with at any length in the mainstream press. Usually these are the positions taken by the two main parties, the Democratic and Republican, roughly corresponding to a moderately liberal view on the one hand and a moderately conservative point of view on the other. Any views that are out of the American mainstream are usually dismissed as insignificant, when not completely ignored.

In principle, however, most journalists agree that all sides of political issues have a right to be heard. The electorate needs to hear a wide variety of political views, and needs access to all relevant information, in order to make the informed decisions on which effective democracy depends. Consequently, few would deny that a national press that only gave one side of political issues, or that only published information favorable to one side or another, would be a bad thing. But, some argue, it is not important that every single news outlet provide that kind of balance, only that all of them, taken together, do so.

That having been said, most of the mainstream news media *do* try to provide some kind of balance in their news coverage of political candidates and issues. Some go even further. They try to provide a balance of editorial opinion as well. They do not, however, try to make that balance absolute. They do not try to present every side of every issue equally. Rather, they attempt to provide what they regard as fair coverage of what they consider to be the most significant sides of major political issues.

This striving after balance is relatively new, however. It is, in fact, contrary to some of the earliest and most honored traditions of the American press. What would such early press (and political) heroes as John Peter Zenger, James and Benjamin Franklin and Tom Paine have thought of this concept of balance? Certainly Zenger would have scoffed at the idea that he owed Governor Cosby a chance to tell his side of the story in the *Journal*. The Franklins would have been outraged at the idea of providing equal space for the Royalists in the *New-England Courant*. These early representatives of the press saw the press not as a dry, neutral observer of the political scene, but as a participant—an advocate of political causes.

This view of the press continued to dominate at least until the advent of the popular press in the mid-nineteenth century. It can be reasonably argued that the later development of the concept of balance came about not so much from an effort to be fair as from a desire to be popular. By attempting to be—or seem—objective, papers could attract readers of all political persuasions.

Is the Press Too Adversarial?

Some politicians feel that the American press is too adversarial toward the government, and toward the politicians who serve in it. They see the press as a swarm of sharks, prowling Washington, D.C. in search of politicians off whom to feed. They say that the hostility of the press makes it more difficult for the government to govern, distracting officials from their real business of running the country.

What is worse, they argue, the adversarial attitude of the press produces a hostile response from the government. When the press treats public officials as enemies, those officials are likely to regard the press as an enemy in return. Fearing that the press will take advantage of any negative information, officials will try to hide as much information as they can from the press. Ironically, then, the determination of the press to discover secrets may actually lead to *more* secrecy within the government rather than less.

But of all the bad effects some politicians see in the adversarial attitude of the press, the worst is its effect on the public. The constant suspicion and hostility toward government expressed in the press, they say, destroy the public's faith in government—a faith that is vital to the health of a democracy. They point to the Watergate case, and to the legacy of suspicion and mistrust of government it left behind. Instead of being the government's adversary, some politicians argue, the press should be the government's ally. Instead of constantly criticizing and complaining, the press should support the policies of the government, helping to explain and justify them to the people.

Most journalists would reply that that describes the role of the press in totalitarian countries—countries in which the press is an arm of the government, and its job is to defend the government against criticism. That is not the traditional role of the press in the United States, nor is it a healthy role for the press in any free and democratic country. In a country like ours, it is the *job* of the press to be critical of the government.

Besides, they argue, they are not sharks. They are

watchdogs. They are the eyes of the public. It is their duty to keep watch on the government, and to give warning of any deception or misuse of power by that government. Like any good watchdog, it is their job to be suspicious. They do not want to feed off politicians, but they do want to keep them honest.

If anything, some journalists would argue, the American press is too docile. Far from being too critical, it is too accepting, too willing to believe and transmit official claims and explanations. The Watergate affair was an isolated instance, and a misleading example of the usual relationship between the government and the press. And even in that case, the great majority of the press proved itself tame and easily manageable by the White House.

In his book *On Press*, journalist Tom Wicker wrote that "most reporters, in 1972, at least suspected that the Watergate break-in had its origins in the White House. . . ." It is likely that few reporters would dispute his assertion. And yet, the vast majority of them failed to pursue the story. They accepted (not privately, but as far as their journalistic efforts were concerned) the official denials of White House involvement. In that case, as in others, Wicker said the press "tended to cooperate in its own deception."

As a result, not only the press but the American public was deceived until well after the election. Far from being too adversarial, history seems to demonstrate, the press is often not adversarial enough.

Is the Press Too Powerful?
There is no question that the American press is enormously powerful. Example after example described in this book has demonstrated that. Its political influence is so great that the press is often referred to as "the

fourth branch of government," as though it were co-equal with the executive, legislative and judicial branches. But, is it *too* powerful? Has the time come to rethink the First Amendment, to limit press freedom and to curb the power of the press?

The First Amendment, after all, was passed at a time when the press consisted largely of weekly news-sheets, read by a relative handful of people. Today, in the age of radio and television news, the press is pervasive, reaching almost everyone in society.

There are some press critics, including those politicians whose careers have been destroyed by revelations in the press, who argue that the press has gotten out of hand. Journalists might respond, however, as Andrew Hamilton argued concerning Governor Cosby in 1735, that it is not the press that destroys politicians' careers, but the politicians themselves. The press only reports what they have done—or what the press believes they have done. Few politicians' careers, if any, have been seriously damaged, much less destroyed, by untrue revelations. Wronged politicians have many avenues for correcting errors, and for replying to any unfair charges made in the press. Most politicians who, like Richard Nixon, have suffered lasting damage from revelations in the press have done so because the revelations were true.

The gravest dangers that many critics see in the power of the press go far beyond the effects of press coverage on the careers of individual politicians. They involve the press's power to sway public opinion on public issues. Clearly that ability gives the press the potential to do tremendous harm. As the great American jurist, Learned Hand, once said: "The hand that rules the press, the radio, the screen and the far-spread magazine rules the country; whether we like it or not, we must learn to accept it." And he went on to explain how the press, misused as a propaganda tool, had the power to bring "civilization to imminent peril of destruction" by indoctrinating an entire population.

"The individual is as helpless against it as the child is helpless against the formulas with which he is indoctrinated." The press can be used, not only "to shape his tastes, his feelings, his desires, and his hopes" but to "convert him into a fanatical zealot, ready to torture and destroy and to suffer mutilation and death. . . ." Clearly the power of the press can be a terribly dangerous thing.

But, supporters of the First Amendment argue, Hand was describing the press in a totalitarian state. It was a captive press that spoke with only one voice: the voice of a dictatorial government. In America—where the freedom of the press is defended by the Constitution, and where the press sees itself more as a critic than as a slave of the government—it is not likely to be used effectively in that way. Here, the press is more likely to be a shield between the people and any government effort to indoctrinate them, than a weapon the government can use against them.

And, is the press really any more powerful today than it was in the past? Is CBS News, for example, really more influential today than Thomas Paine was when he called for the American colonies to rebel against England? Or William Randolph Hearst when he called for war against Spain? It would be hard to argue that it is.

Besides, say its defenders, the press is not nearly as able to influence public opinion as many people believe. Far from being the leader of national opinion, the press is primarily a reflector of it. A prominent newspaper editor once said that the art of writing a good editorial was not telling the people what they *ought* to think, but telling them what they already thought.

On the other hand, even the press's strongest defenders would not claim that it has no power to influence opinion at all. Nor would they argue that it has never abused its power, or that it never would. But, they say, the best antidote to any abuse of power on the part of one element of the press is the counteracting effect of other elements of the press. For that reason, it is freedom of the press itself, and not any curtailment of its freedom, that offers the best defense against abuses by the press.

Someone must make decisions about what will be published in the media. Those decisions will inevitably determine much of what the people of the country will know—and what they will not know. Press freedom helps assure that those decisions will be made by a variety of private individuals and organizations, each with different perspectives and political beliefs. Presumably, they will disagree with each other, and compete with each other. Ideally, they will publish a wide range of information and arguments, on the basis of which the people will be able to make their own judgments.

The alternative is to give the decision of what the people will be allowed to know to the government. Rather than getting a variety of information on which to base their political judgments, the people would have only the information the government wants them to have. By controlling what the people know, the government would be able to control, to a large extent, what the people think. That, the defenders of press freedom say, is a recipe for despotism and tyranny.

Ultimately, as associate justice of the Supreme Court, Felix Frankfurter, put it, "Freedom of the press is not an end in itself but a means to the end of a free society." Some would argue that it is more than just *a* means; it is the most important means to such a free society.

Among them would be Thomas Jefferson. Despite the vicious personal attacks he suffered from the press, he remained a champion of the First Amendment. He knew better than most the harm that could be done by a corrupt and unscrupulous press. And yet, he believed, the press must be protected, even in the "right of lying and calumniating."

Some people today feel that there should be a kind of compromise, a way to curb the unscrupulous press while offering freedom to those elements of the press who are accurate and fair. But, as Jefferson understood nearly two centuries ago, the First Amendment was passed to protect a fiercely partisan and combative press, not a moderate and timid one. If press freedom is to be protected, *all* the press must be protected, not just that which acts responsibly. Press abuse, Jefferson said, is "an evil for which there is no remedy, our liberty depends on the freedom of the press, and that cannot be limited without being lost."

For Further Reading

For those interested in the history of American journalism, the following overview of that subject (up to 1960) is highly recommended:

Mott, Frank Luther, *American Jouranlism*, New York: The Macmillan Company, 1962.

For a vision of the Watergate affair from the journalist's perspective, what could be better than the account of the reporters who broke the story:

Bernstein, Carl, and Bob Woodward. *All the President's Men*, New York: Simon and Schuster, 1974.

The following all deal with varying aspects of the subject of the relationship between politics and the press:

Arlen, Michael J. *The Living Room War*. New York: The Viking Press, 1969.

Pollard, James. *The Presidents and the Press*. New York: Macmillan, 1947.

Halberstam, David. *The Powers That Be*. New York: Alfred A. Knopf, 1979.

Hohenberg, John. *A Crisis for the American Press*. Columbia University Press, 1978.

Leamer, Laurence. *The Paper Revolutionaries: The Rise of the Underground Press*. New York: Simon and Schuster, 1972.

Minor, Dale. *The Information War*. New York: Hawthorne Books, 1970.

Knightley, Phillip. *The First Casualty*. New York: Harcourt Brace Jovanovich, 1975.

Wicker, Tom. *On Press*. New York: The Viking Press, 1978.

Wiggins, J. Russell. *Freedom or Secrecy?* New York: Oxford University Press, 1964.

Index